On The Rocks

Marriage and Margaritas

Erika Daniels

EXPLORA BOOKS
700 – 838 West Hastings St. Vancouver, BC V6C 0A6
www.explorabooks.com
Phone: (604) 330 6795

Because of the dynamic nature of the Internet, any web addresses or links contained in this book may have changed since publication and may no longer be valid. The views expressed in this work are solely those of the author and do not necessarily reflect the views of the publisher, and the publisher hereby disclaims any responsibility for them.

ISBN: 978-1-998394-66-1

ON THE Rocks

Marriage and Margaritas

Erika Daniels

Chapter 1

*I*t is a hot, sunny Saturday in May, Cinco de Mayo. Our friends Marcus and Janet are having a party to celebrate, though neither of them is the least bit Spanish. Janet spent a summer in Mexico during college, and could speak some broken language, but Marcus is as Norwegian as a clog. It is an annual event and always a good time. Marcus' homemade salsa, Janet's fresh guacamole, margaritas, grilled chicken, Coronas.

When we arrive, Janet rolls out the front door like a little burst of energy.

"Hola, Senor Brian and Seniorita Erika!" she shouts at us. "Ready for a fiesta?!"

"Si," I shout back, with one of the dozen Spanish words I know. We smile at each other. I feel like we should kiss each other's cheeks like they do in Mexico when they greet each other.

"I've been waiting for you to get here to have a margarita," she says.

"Well, let's get going!" I tell her.

Before I know it, I have a drink in my hand. Marcus and my husband, Brian, are outside supervising the chicken on the grill. "Can you help me with the guacamole?" Janet asks.

"Sure," I say, even though I hate the stuff and really could just do without it. "What do you want me to do?"

She hands me a knife and pushes a cutting board and vegetables toward me. I get started while we chat about our kids and jobs, this and that. I finish up with the vegetables and slam my drink. "Done!" I shout.

"Me too!," she says.

Minutes later we are on round two. Before I know it, guests are arriving and Janet is busy greeting everyone. I start mixing drinks and organizing the food table while she socializes. I love that about her. She is such a gracious hostess and makes everyone feel so welcome. The men are hanging out in the garage, and most of the women come inside and congregate in the kitchen. I am so busy making margaritas by then that I don't even have time to drink my own. When things slow down in the kitchen, I make my way out to the garage to see what is going on out there.

As I open the door to the garage, I almost plant a kiss on the face of a pretty, young, blonde. She is followed by her very handsome husband, Cole, who I have known all my life. I have never met his wife though. Her name is Shelley.

"Oh, sorry about that!" I say, grinning widely.

"No problem," she replies, and smiles warmly back. Cole smiles too.

"Hey, Erika. How's it goin'?" he says.

"I'm good! The margaritas are going down like water. Just going out to check on the guys in the garage," I say.

I wink at them as they head into the house together, holding hands. Ah, young love, I think to myself. How cute. I suppose I am a bit envious. Brian and I have been together long enough that we are over that phase. We met when I was 17 and he was 18. I was still in high school and he was in college. He is my one and only love, my one and only sexual partner. We have a healthy sex life and a passionate marriage, since we are both very strong-willed and obstinate, which makes for fireworks both in and out of the bedroom. But I miss the romantic love that we used to have; writing love notes, stealing kisses, holding hands in public.

A few minutes later, Cole and Shelley come out of the house, still holding hands and Shelley holding a margarita. They both sit down at the table next to me.

"So, I'm Shelley," she says, holding a hand out to introduce herself.

"Erika. Nice to meet you," I say, shaking it limply. It's always strange to me when a woman shakes my hand outside of work functions. We sit and chat for a long time, mostly Shelley and I, while Cole watches

us. We talk about our kids. I tell her we have two boys and a girl. She tells me that they have two boys. She tells me she got pregnant before they were married, just like me. We talk about our jobs. She does in-home daycare. I have a 15-year career in healthcare. She went to a

big high school. I went to high school in the boondocks. Her parents are divorced. Mine have been married for over 30 years. She has a sister. I have a brother (and another half-sister that I don't mention). On the surface, we have very little in common really, but there is chemistry between us that makes the conversation flow. I excuse myself after a while and go in the house to get another drink. The garage and the house are full of people; family and neighbors, friends from work, and some others I haven't met yet. On my way back out to the garage, I catch Brian stealing a glance at me. I smile. I love little moments like that. I head over by him.

"Whattya lookin' at," I chirp with a grin.

"Nothing," he says with a smile.

That's our usual banter. We stand there for a few minutes and watch the crowd together. As I'm walking away, I turn around and catch him staring at my ass. He smirks at me. I need another drink, and I notice that Shelley does too. I stop by and ask if she wants another one. She nods her head and I grab her glass and head into the house. When I come back, it feels like it got darker outside or maybe I'm just drunk. The crowd has thinned out a bit too. I hand Shelley her margarita and stand beside her. Brian and Cole are both watching us from different sides of the room. I would love to know what those two are thinking. Never mind, I'm pretty sure I already do.

Janet comes out from the house and waves me over. She asks if I'll make a couple more margaritas for some friends of hers that just got there. I tell Shelley I'll be right back and head into the house. I make the first margaritas, then a couple more. I stir the food and wipe up the counters. Then out the front picture window of the house, I see Cole and

Shelley walking to their car. I excuse myself and hurry after them. I have no idea what I'm going to say when I get there, but I at least want to say goodbye. As they're getting in their car, I take off running.

When I get to the car, I am winded and probably look like an idiot. "Hey, you're leaving already," I ask, breathlessly.

"Yeah, we just had a sitter for a couple of hours so we have to head home," Cole says from the driver's seat.

I lean over and look at Shelley and ask, "Would you guys like to come over some time with the kids and just hang out?"

What am I saying? That is so not like me. But I feel like it's time for Brian and I to branch out a little, make some new friends, outside of the usual family and high school friends that we still hang out with. I guess I'm getting a little bored.

"Sure," Shelley says. Her eyes light up. "That sounds great." "What about next weekend?" I ask.

"Well, Cole has to play softball Friday night and he has to work a side job on Saturday," she replies.

"Where does he play softball," I ask.

"Down in Monroe," she says.

Perfect. Monroe is a town of about 100 people only 5 miles from our house. There are 2 bars, a restaurant and a gas station, but not much else. If it weren't for the creamery in town, it probably wouldn't even exist. And of course, in the boondocks, there is a softball field.

"Well, what if you come out for dinner before softball on Friday?" I suggest.

They look at each other and shrug their shoulders.

"Yeah, that sounds good," Shelley says while Cole smiles. "What time are you thinking?"

"Maybe around 5?" I offer. "Brian will probably work from home and I'm off on Fridays so we'll have time to get things ready during the day."

"Well, my daycare kids don't leave until 5 so we probably can't be there until closer to 5:30," she says.

"Sounds perfect," I say. I look at Cole. "You know where we live, right?"

"Yeah, the big yellow house that borders the minimum maintenance on County Road 23, right?" he says.

"Do you want me to bring anything," Shelley asks.

"Nope, just yourselves. See you then!" I say, as Cole puts the car into drive.

I step back from the car and wave as they drive away. It feels good to do something different. I'm happy that we're going to have some company over and excited at the thought of making some new friends.

Chapter 2

*T*he week goes by fast. Brian and I decide to make steaks and potatoes on the grill, with fresh steamed broccoli, lettuce salad and a fruit salad for the kids, and beer for dessert, of course. When they get to our house, our 4-year-old daughter Becca greets them at the front door with her face pressed up against the glass. The little stinker, I just cleaned that today.

"Hi there," I say. "Come on in!"

As they step into our house, Cole is holding a 12-pack of beer. They seem taken over by the house for a moment. The living room, dining room and kitchen are a wide open space, and you can see most of it from the front door. There are large windows facing a wrap-around porch, another huge window in the dining room and more windows in the kitchen facing east, that overlook the deck and the rest of our 40 acres. It's really nothing fancy, but the house is around 5,000 square feet and bigger than many homes in the area. When I found the home plan online, it was designed to have three bedrooms for the kids upstairs, but our oldest son Bryce wanted all of us to be together on the main floor so we had the plan modified a bit. I give them the tour of the upstairs. The kids take them through their bedrooms, excited to "show off" their space. I walk them to our master bedroom and bath. There is a door from our bedroom that leads out to the same deck that is shared with the patio door from the kitchen. We head outside. From the deck we can see the plot lines where our new pool is going to be started in a few weeks. Brian describes the size, the shape, the concrete patio that will surround it. By the looks on their faces they seem overwhelmed with it all. I offer them a beer.

Cole and Shelley smile.

"Sure," they say in unison, looking at each other.

The three of them stay on the deck and chat. I head downstairs with a beer tray, Becca following closely behind. She is holding on to the wall for balance, leaving fingerprints behind all the way. She helps me load the beer on the tray and we head back upstairs. They are all in the kitchen now, talking about the land. Brian is pointing out the window, showing them where our property ends and begins. Shelley is holding Reid, and Cory is tagging behind her. Their boys are adorable. Cory is 3 and looks just like his Dad. He is a very handsome little boy, with pudgy red cheeks, even in the cool air of spring. Reid is their younger son. He is 9 months and very active. He looks more like Shelley, but I can definitely tell that they are brothers. Brian goes out the patio door to check the food on the grill. The table is already set. The salads are on. Becca's old high chair is ready for Reid. Cory and Becca will share the bench. There are enough chairs for the rest of us.

Brian hollers in from the deck, "Steaks are coming off the grill." That means I have 5 minutes to finish up the rest of the meal. He likes to let the steaks sit a while before we eat. He says it's good to let them fester. That is one thing we are good at. We have actually learned to cook well together. I smile because I love that about us. I start the broccoli to steam.

"Time for another beer," I ask?

Becca runs to the beer tray on the counter. She loves to be our waitress. Even at 4-years-old, she already seems like a little housewife.

She loves to cook and clean, and dote on guests. Before they answer, she brings them one anyway.

"She is such a sweetheart. I want a little girl," she says, looking over at Cole. He looks away.

"No way," he says. "Two is enough."

"Well, she can be a little naughty too," I tell them. "And she's got a mind of her own. Her baby song is 'Miss Independent.'" "Oh, that's cute," Shelley says.

"Are you ready?" Brian asks.

"Yep, just need to get the broccoli on the table," I tell him. I call the kids upstairs and we all sit down for dinner. Cole and Shelley are both very conversational. I like that about them. I notice Cole watching her as she talks. He seems just genuinely fond of her. It makes me sentimental. I wonder if Brian looks at me that way when I'm not looking. At 6:30, Cole is suddenly in a hurry to finish eating.

"I better get going," he says.

"What time is softball?" I ask.

"6:45," he says.

"Well, why don't you guys go ahead," I say, looking at Brian then Cole. "We'll get the kids cleaned up and head down in a bit." "Sounds good to me," Brian says. He is just glad he doesn't have to help with the dishes.

Brian and Cole get up from the table and head to the mudroom. Becca wants to go with them but I make her stay with us. The husbands are out the door and before I know it they are headed down the driveway in a cloud of dust in Brian's truck.

I decide to leave the dishes on the table, which is so not like me. I figure I can clean up when we get home later. We load the kids up in Cole and Shelley's mini-van and head down the driveway. When we get to Monroe, the game has already started. Brian has a beer in his hand. I am jealous, pissed off that I forgot to bring any. Cole's Dad, Sal, offers Shelley and me a beer.

"Of course, I would love a beer," I tell him. "Thank you, sir," as I grab it from his hand.

We have a few beers as we watch the softball game and the kids run around the ball field. At the end of the game, I ask if they'd all like to come back to our house for a beer. When we get home, we sit in the living room and chat. Cole's parents leave after about an hour, and Cole and Shelley stay. When the beer tray is empty, Cole offers to get some more in the basement. He grabs the tray and heads toward the steps. I notice that he is slurring his words a little, and he fumbles as he rounds the corner of the staircase. The next thing we know, Cole is bouncing off the side of the staircase walls and tumbling down the stairs.

"Jeezzus, Cole," Shelley says. "Are you drunk?"

I'm trying not to laugh, and then realize that he might be hurt, for goodness sakes.

"Are you OK?" I ask, as I get up off the couch and head over to the top of the stairs.

"Yeah, I'm fine," he says, looking up at me.

I can tell that his ego is a little bruised. He had a beer in his hand on the way down. The walls are wet with beer, and the beer can is lying at his feet at the bottom of the steps. He managed to land standing up. "Will you get me a rag so I can clean it up?" he asks. "Hell no," I say. "I got it. You just get the beer." "I don't think he needs any more beer," Shelley says.

"Oh yes, he does," I say. "He's not going to make that kind of mess in my house and not have another beer to celebrate." We all laugh together. We have one more beer, but it's getting late, almost midnight. Reid is sleeping on his mama's chest, and Cory is getting crabby. Our boys are in the basement watching TV now, and Becca won't sleep until they leave. Shelley stands up.

"Well, we better get going," she says.

Cole's drunk stare is fixed on her. He's giving her the brown puppy dog eyes because he doesn't want to leave.

"C'mon," she says. "Get up."

When he stands up, she starts to hand him their sleeping baby boy.

"Now don't drop him," she says with a smile.

I laugh.

"So you guys want to do this again sometime?" I ask.

"Hell yeah," Shelley says.

Cole is already on his way out the front door. He almost stumbles again on the way out. Shelley and I exchange phone numbers. We walk them out to their car and wave as they head down the driveway.

"Well, that was fun," I say to Brian, when we're walking back in the house.

"Yeah, I'm glad they came over," he said.

For a moment, I'm proud of myself for stepping outside my comfort zone, and hoping that we really do get together again sometime soon.

Chapter 3

*I*n the next couple of weeks, we're busy with the end of the school year and the contractor is digging ground for the pool. It's going to take six weeks to build, but should be done by the Fourth of July. Since I invited Cole and Shelley over the first time, I wait to hear from them. I don't want to be too over the top.

Shelley finally calls on the Saturday of Memorial Day weekend. "Hello," I answer, not recognizing the number.

"Hey, it's Shelley," she says. "How've you been?" "Good, how 'bout you?" I say.

"We're good. Cole is working today but we were wondering if you want to get together tomorrow for a few beers and maybe grill out again or something?" she asks.

"Sounds good to me," I say. "We have no plans."

"We'll bring chicken and hot dogs to grill," she says.

"No, no, no," I protest. "We have a whole freezer full of meat. Why don't you bring some beer and a salad? Come over about 3 and we'll eat around 5. Sound good?"

"Yep, sounds good. See you then," she says as we hang up. I find Brian downstairs and tell him about our plans.

"Do you want me to see if Marcus and Janet wanna come over too?" he asks.

We haven't really seen them since the Cinco de Mayo party almost a month ago, which ended with Marcus drunk off his ass and talking like a big shot. He irritates me when he gets so drunk. He and I are like fire and gasoline at times. We ended on a bit of a sour note that night, with me telling him to shut up and go to bed. I tolerate him because he is one of Brian's best friends, and Janet is one of mine, but there are times when I just can't keep my mouth shut.

"Sure," I grunt as I walk away, secretly hoping that they can't make it.

As I head upstairs, I can hear him on the phone with Marcus. They're chatting away like a couple of teenage girls. Fifteen minutes later, he hollers up the stairs that they're joining us. I hope Marcus is on his best behavior.

The next afternoon, Marcus and Janet arrive first. Their girls, Jenna and Amy, are 5 and 1, and complete opposites. Jenna is our goddaughter. She looks like Marcus, with big brown eyes on a wide face with tan complexion, and a short, stocky body. Jenna shares the same birthday as our oldest son, Bryce, so we've celebrated their birthdays together since Jenna was born. Amy is a toe-head, with blond hair but big brown eyes too. She has a fair complexion and a petite build, more like Janet's family. She is a jabber-jaw, but I can't understand anything that she says just yet.

Jenna heads downstairs to hang out. She is a bit of a tomboy. She loves to watch our boys, Bryce and Bennett, play Xbox, and that's mostly what the kids do when their family comes over. Amy is attached at the hip to Janet. She is already driving her crazy. Marcus grabs her and picks her up, tickling her until she is giggling. I open a bottle of wine for Janet and me to share. Brian gets the two of them a beer. We walk out on the deck and look at the hole in the ground. The pool is coming along. They are surprised at how fast things are moving. We start talking about plans for the Fourth of July. We usually throw some money together for a fireworks show at their house, but this year we decide we're going to have it our house so we can enjoy the pool too.

I see a car slowing down on the highway and pulling into the field drive.

"Cole and Shelley are here," I say, getting up from my chair to meet them at the door.

Brian stays on the deck with Marcus and Janet.

"Hey," I say, opening the door as they are walking up the steps.

"How are ya?"

"Ready for a beer," Cole says, flashing me his infectious smile. He sets Reid down and goes back to the car to get a case of beer. Cory is following behind him. Hearing voices, he heads toward the stairs, sliding down all the way on his butt.

I leave the front door open for Cole, and we head to the kitchen. "Do you want some wine, or are you having beer?" I ask. "I'll have some wine," she says.

I pour her a glass and we head out to the deck.

"Hello, Shelley," Janet says politely, but a little awkwardly. She is usually so warm, friendly.

Shelley says hello. There is a moment of silence that is uncomfortable. Then Cole strolls out through the patio door, approaches Marcus and gives him a high-five. Their dads are first cousins, so they are family. We sit and chat, talking about the progress on the pool again so Cole and Shelley have the latest news. I want to change the subject but Janet goes on and on about the size and the depth and the concrete pad, and this and that. Then we're talking about the contractors, and the timing. Brian warns me that the chicken is almost done, so I head in the house to put the rest of dinner on the table. Janet joins me, leaving Shelley sitting out on the deck with the men. I don't really know what it is, but I'm getting this feeling that Janet doesn't really like her.

When we sit down for dinner, I realize that I have the high chair set up for Reid but Amy usually uses it when Marcus and Janet come for dinner. Janet doesn't even give it a thought when she picks Amy up and squeezes her into the chair. Shelley is watching her. So is Brian. He looks at me. First come, first serve, I guess. It bothers me, but I don't know what else to do. Shelley holds Reid throughout dinner, as he squirms and fidgets. Janet doesn't even seem to notice, which is one thing that really bothers me about her at times. She can be so damn selfish, a little oblivious to the world around her. A little narcissistic, I guess.

When we finish eating, the four older kids head back downstairs. Amy and Reid stay with us, while Becca pretends that she is their babysitter. About 10 o'clock, Janet tells Marcus she is ready to head home, that she has a lot to get done the next day before heading back to work on Tuesday. That is so not like her, I think to myself, but say nothing. As usual, Marcus does not want to leave, but finally does when she begs him at 10:30. Cole and Shelley go home at 11:30. I decide that it's probably best not to mix that group together ever again.

Chapter 4

A few weeks later, it's Flowerfest, a festival held every year on Father's Day weekend in the town where Brian grew up. We usually go out Friday or Saturday night, then go to the parade on Sunday and head downtown for the carnival afterward. Later we watch softball games at the park in town.

Shelley sends me a text Thursday night to see if we have plans.

Hey there

Hey

Going out this weekend?

Yep, not sure which night though.

We're having a little get-together Saturday night if you want to come over.

Sure

What should I bring?

An appetizer

What time

Whenever after 6, Cole is playing softball all day, kids are going to his parent's house.

Sounds good, see you then.

On Friday, I call Janet and ask if she and Marcus want to go along to the party with us, but she politely declines. That's strange, not like her to want to miss Flowerfest. Later I tell Brian about the invite. He thinks it sounds good, so Saturday night we head to Cole and Shelley's house around 7. They are a lot younger than us. Cole is 28 and she is 25. Most of the crowd at the party is under 30. We only know about half the people there, but we stay until 9 and then head uptown for the street dance. When we're leaving, Shelley says that they'll be up after a bit. When we get to the dance, I lose Brian right away. I'm wandering around, chatting with friends and people I haven't seen in ages. Before I know it, I'm drunk and it's after midnight. I finally run into Brian in the middle of the street. He's talking to Shelley, alone.

"Hey," I say. "Where've you been all night?"

"I was over at the Legion talking to Ted, and then I ran into Doug over at the liquor store," he tells us.

Shelley stands there and smiles. I am cautious about what I am going to say. For some reason, for the first time since I met her, I realize that I'm not sure if I should trust her alone with my husband.

"Well, I think we should get heading home, since I have to drive," I say.

"Ok," Brian says, disappointed.

I turn to Shelley.

"Do you know where Cole is?" I ask.

She looks puzzled.

"No, I haven't seen him all night," she says. "We're having an after bar if you guys want to come over later."

"No, but thanks," I reply. "I think we're going to head home."

Brian looks pissed. I can tell that he wants to stay. I figure I can make it up to him later. Shelley turns to leave.

"OK, well whatever. You're more than welcome to come over. Text me later if you want to," she says as she's walking away. In that moment, I'm not sure if the "text me later" is directed at me or Brian. I turn and look at him but say nothing more about it.

"Ready to go?" I ask.

"Sure," he lies.

Our car is parked way down by the ball fields by Cole and Shelley's house. We start walking and get about halfway there before I decide I need to say something.

"So what was that all about?" I ask.

"What do you mean?" Brian replies.

"What were you and Shelley talking about?" I ask.

"She just asked if she could have my cell phone number in case she needs to get in touch with me sometime," he says.

"And you gave it to her," I said.

"Yeah, why?" he asks, raising his voice.

"Well, I don't really know why she would need your cell phone number," I say.

He grabs my hand, hard.

"It's not that big of deal, Erika" he says. "If you want me to, I'll delete it."

After he offers, I shake my head.

"No, that's OK. You're right," I say. "It's not that big of deal." We keep walking. When we get to the ball park, it is really dark. There are no street lights on and it starts to rain. Brian is still holding my hand when it starts to rain harder. He looks at me and we both start running. Our car is just on the other side of one of the dugouts. When we get inside the dugout, he pulls me close to him and kisses me on the mouth. Hmm, I shudder. I am cold now from the rain, but the idea of making out in a dugout turns me on. I grab him in the ass and pull him into me, letting him know what I have in mind. He puts his hands around both sides of my face and kisses me harder. He kisses my neck and I turn around and push my ass into his groin. I can feel that he is hard. He puts his hands over my boobs and fondles them, then pulls my shirt out of my shorts and reaches his hands up under my shirt, cupping them in his hands. His hands move down inside my shorts, but he can't quite reach where he really wants to be. He turns me back around and then pushes his hand down deeper, pressing his finger over my clit. I feel like we are teenagers again. I am breathing harder, then out of breath.

"What do you want to do," I say. "I want to lick you," he requests.

"Right here," I say? "Are you kidding me?"

But the thought of it turns me on. He answers when he pushes me until the backs of my legs are touching the bench. He unbuttons my shorts and they slip down my legs. I grab for them before they hit the ground, reminding myself that it is filthy on the floor of a dugout. Sunflower seeds, chew spit, gum. My mind wanders for a moment. Looking at him, I set my shorts on the bench. He takes my left leg and lifts it up to rest there, so I am wide open for him. Luckily I am wearing a thong. He grabs the pink fabric in the middle and pushes it aside as he bends over and licks me the first time. I gasp. I cannot believe we are doing this. I look around, wondering if anybody is watching. I close my eyes then, trying to put it out of mind. He holds my thong and laps his tongue over me, again and again. He is an expert with me by now. For 10 minutes, he brings me closer and closer until I can feel myself starting to orgasm. Then I hear voices.

"Shit," I say.

I open my eyes and look around. There are two figures coming toward us across the ball field, staggering a little and laughing, loudly, a woman and a man. We stay there, motionless. I am trying to not laugh out loud, hoping that it isn't someone that we know, but knowing that it probably is. They turn toward the other dugout then, walk past it, and out into the street.

Brian returns to me but my orgasm is already gone.

"I lost it," I tell him.

He knows what I mean. I put my leg down. He grabs my hand as I stumble, drunk.

"Turn around," he whispers at me, his breath smelling like beer and chew.

I turn and bend over, knowing what he wants. I grab the bench with both hands to hold on. He presses his cock into me, slowly, and then moving faster and harder until my head is pushing against the hard siding. I put my hands up on the cold steel to brace myself. It is still raining lightly and the air is cold. I hold on there until he orgasms. My legs are shaking when he pulls out of me from holding that pose for so long. I reach for my shorts but I can't find them. They fell on the ground. Brian picks them up and hands them to me and I smile. My God, we are reckless sometimes. He grabs my hand and we walk around the side of the dugout to where our car is parked.

"I think we should just hang out here for a little while. I'm too drunk to drive right now," I say. "Let's just get our chairs out of the back of the car and sleep for a few hours. Then we can get up and go home." "Alright," he says.

With two DUIs already on his record, Brian knows he can't drive either, so we get our chairs and fall asleep until 4:30. When I wake up, the birds are starting to chirp. I'm not sober yet but it isn't bar close either, so I wake Brian up and drive us home.

Chapter 5

By Fourth of July weekend the pool is finally done. I can't believe the summer is already half gone. I want to have a party to celebrate. Brian talks to Marcus late in the week and they decide they are going to pick up fireworks on Saturday morning. We decide to shoot them off at our house this year so we can hang by the pool, grill out and then do the fireworks when the sun goes down. I send a text to Shelley to ask if their family wants to join us. Marcus and Janet invite some other friends of ours too. Everyone comes over around 2 that day. Brian's cousin Ted and his wife and 3 kids, my parents, Marcus' sister and her family, our friends Gary and Julie, Dave, and Cole's sister, Jenny. The kids are enjoying the pool, and the adults are enjoying some ice cold beverages. Around 4, I head into the house to get things started for dinner. As I'm walking up the stairs, I turn around to ask if anyone needs anything when I come back. I notice Cole staring at my ass. I smile and he smiles back.

"Lookin' good," he says, as I turn back around and head up the stairs. Goodness, what the hell was that.

Janet follows me inside. She is quiet today. I wonder what is going on. Our friendship has changed in the last couple of months. I don't really know why. I feel like every time I try to reach out to her she just isn't interested in doing anything with us.

"Is everything ok with you," I ask?

"Yes, why?" she replies.

It's not like her to be short with me.

"I don't know. You just don't seem like yourself lately," I say. She pauses. I can tell that whatever she's going to say is not going to be easy.

"Well, I don't really know how to say this nicely, so I'm just going to say it. There's another side of Shelley that I'm not really sure about," she says.

"What do you mean," I ask.

"I don't know. I just think you should be careful around her," she says, as she looks at me and then heads back outside. I watch her for a moment. What the hell. What is she, jealous? I follow her outside but keep my distance. I don't really know what to think about what she just said to me.

When the sun goes down, the guys get the fireworks going. It's a fantastic 45-minute show. Not bad for a bunch of folks living in the boondocks. It's no surprise that Janet wants to leave right after the fireworks are over. Everyone else leaves too, except Cole, Shelley, and Cole's sister. Jenny mentions that there is a great band down at Harper's that night and wonders if we want to go. Brian just wants to stay home, Cole too, but Shelley and I want to go. I've been in my swimwear all day and my hair is a mess.

"I'll have to shower before we go," I say.

"Well, hurry up and get going," Jenny says.

"Alright," I say, looking at Brian. "Are you sure you're OK with this?" I don't want him to throw it in my face tomorrow. "Yeah, go, it's fine," he says, convincing me. "Cole and I will stay here with the kids."

I head upstairs and hop in the shower. I'm going to leave my hair wet and let it dry on the way. As I'm getting dressed, I notice Cole standing out on the deck watching me. I move away from the window. Then Shelley comes over to the door. It's locked, but she knocks and peers in. What in the hell possessed me to put a patio door off my bedroom? I'm in my shirt and underwear. I grab some shorts and throw them on before I walk over and open the door.

"Ready?" she says, as she steps in.

"Yep, just about," I say. "I just need to throw some makeup on." "You look fine," she says, as she lies down across the bed. "Whatever," I say.

I walk in the bathroom and put on some mascara and lipstick. I throw a couple of other things in a bag that I can put on in the car. I go back in the bedroom. She looks so comfortable it makes me want to lie down, so I do. We're laying there next to each other on the bed saying nothing at all and all of a sudden I feel uncomfortable. I hope that she doesn't think that I mean anything by it.

"Couldn't you just lay here all night," she says.

Umm, not sure what that's supposed to mean.

"Well, if I lay here any longer, I'm going to fall asleep," I tell her, popping up off the bed. "We better get going."

She gets up too. Jenny is standing outside on the deck waiting for us. I opt myself out of driving and Shelley says that she can drive so we get in her car and take off. No husbands, no kids, just freedom.

On the way in the car, Shelley tells us she has a new song that she wants to play for us. It's Bubbly, by Colbie Caillat.

It starts in my toes, make me crinkles my nose Wherever it goes I always know that you make me smile, please stay for a while now Just take your time, wherever you go.

Jenny and I both love it. She plays it all the way there. When we get to the bar, it's packed. When we walk in, Shelley immediately walks up to a kid that has always been kind of a punk to me. Jenny and I walk to the bar and get a beer. Before I know it, Shelley is gone. Jenny says she saw her leave with the punk. After about an hour, they aren't back yet. What the hell is going on, I'm thinking. If I were Jenny, I'd be a little worried that my sister-in-law left with some guy over an hour ago and they're nowhere to be found, but it doesn't seem to be a big deal to her. After two hours, she's worried.

"Well, where in the hell do you think they went?" she asks. "I don't know," I say. "We could take a walk through the campground and look for them."

Near the bar, there is a campground with about 100 campsites. Jenny wonders if maybe they decided to take a walk around the campground and visit some of the campers or something. As we make our way outside, Justin and Shelley walk over from the other side of the parking lot.

"Where've you been?" Jenny asks.

"We were talking over by Justin's car," Shelley says, trying to blow it off.

Um, not cool, I'm thinking.

"I think it's time to head home," Jenny says.

"Why," Shelley says.

"Well, it's almost midnight and you've been gone like all night," Jenny says.

I can tell she is pissed. Shelley turns and looks at Justin. "OK, well, I guess we're going to head home," she says. "Ok, well, see ya," he says as he starts walking back toward the bar.

When we get in the car, Jenny is all over her.

"I don't think it's too cool that you were gone for over 2 hours talking to Justin," she says to Shelley.

"Why?" Shelley asks. "We were just talking." "Well, why couldn't you talk in the bar?" Jenny asks.

"I don't know. We just went for a walk. That's it," she says. Jenny says nothing until we get a couple of miles from town. "Can you just take me home? I'll get my car tomorrow," Jenny says.

"Yeah," Shelley says, appearing unconcerned that Jenny is mad. I'm sitting in the backseat, just observing. Great, now they're both pissed off. We drop Jenny off at home and head to my house.

When we get there, Cole and Brian are drinking out on the patio and the kids are in the house. Becca and Reid are sleeping. Bryce, Bennett and Cory are watching a movie. We sit outside for a little bit. It's hot, sticky, humid. Brian hasn't closed the pool yet and I feel like swimming. I stand up to go upstairs.

"Where are you going," Brian hollers after me.

"I'm going to get my suit on," I tell him.

"Right now?" he asks.

"Yeah, it's hot, and I didn't swim all day," I remind him. I go upstairs and put my suit on. When I come back down to the pool, Shelley is in hers too. I head over to the pool and start to step in. It's so warm, almost too warm for the outside air. Shelley follows me in.

"Ooh, it's really warm," I say.

"Is it?" Brian asks, a sly grin on his face.

If we were alone, we'd be naked. We hadn't christened the pool yet.

"Come on in," I tell him, smiling.

He stands up and walks over. He dips his foot in. Shelley is on the other end of the pool.

"Oh, that is warm," he confirms.

Brian slips off his shirt. Cole takes a drink of his beer, watching us. Cole stands up and slips off his shirt and heads to the other end of the pool, where Shelley is standing. Brian walks in slowly, getting to his junk, then utters something under his breath and pauses. He walks a little closer to me until the water is up to his chest. I reach behind my back and undo my bikini top, letting it roll off as my boobs fall forward. My nipples are hard, erect. I'm watching Brian as he gets closer to me and then covers my boobs so Cole and Shelley can't see them. The lights flicker in the house and I turn to see if the kids are coming out. It's nothing, just the TV. I look over by Shelley. Cole is in the pool already and they are kissing. She turns away from us, and Cole unhooks her top too. Brian and I are turning in circles, kissing, and he is rubbing my nipples. All of the outside lights on the house are off so it is mostly dark. We can't really see each other, but just moving shadows. Brian and I stand there close for a few minutes and then I turn and dive past him. When I come up through the water, I stand straight up, taller than the water, and the lights from inside the house turn brighter and shine right on my chest. When I look toward the house, Bryce is standing at the sliding glass door. I slide under the water, then look around for my bikini top in case he comes outside.

"What are you guys doing," he yells out into the darkness. "We're just swimming, buddy," Brian says.

"In the dark," he asks?

"Yes, in the dark," Brian says.

He walks back to the couch, and we're all laughing then. Shit. That was a close one.

Chapter 6

A few weeks later, I get a text from Shelley while I'm on my way home from work. I've been texting and talking with her on the phone a few times, but we've been busy with other stuff and we haven't really seen each other.

What's going on tonight?

      Volleyball. How bout you?

Cole's gonna watch the kids

      Mind if I cum watch

Sure, whatever. Drinks afterwards?

      What time does it start?

645

      C u later then?

Yep

Great, that will be fun. After a while, I get tired of hanging out with the volleyball crew, especially toward the end of the summer. And Shelley and I don't get a lot of time together, just the two of us, so I am looking forward to it. By the time I get home with the kids, Brian is already there making dinner. We finish eating and I rush to get ready for volleyball. Before I leave, I give Brian a quick kiss and holler out a "love you" as I head out the door. I tell him that Shelley is coming to volleyball so I might be a little later. He rolls his eyes and tells me to call if I need a ride home.

It's hot that night. I love the heat. By 7:15, Shelley still isn't there and I'm starting to get worried. I'm sure everything is fine, but between games I text her to make sure.

Still coming to volleyball?

I keep checking my phone, wondering why she hasn't responded, trying to not worry. On the way into the Legion, I get a call from home.

"Hello?" I say.

"Hi, Mom," hearing Bryce's voice on the other end of the line. "Hi, babe. What's up?" I ask.

"Nothing," he says, quietly.

"What are you doing?" I ask.

"Just sitting downstairs watching TV," I tell him.

"Where are your brother and sister?" I ask.

"Bennett is here watching TV with me. Becca's upstairs," he says. "Where's your Dad?" I ask.

"He's outside on the deck," he says.

I pause.

"What's he doing out there?" I ask.

"He's sitting out there with Shelley," he tells me.

"What? What do you mean? What are they doing?" I ask, my voice sounding concerned.

"I don't know. They're just sitting up there having some beers and Shelley is smoking," he says, trying to reassure me.

It's funny that he mentions the smoking because I know he hates it. "Well, that's weird," I say. "She was going to come to volleyball tonight. Does she have the boys with her?" "No, she's by herself," he says.

"Oh, ok," I say.

"What time are you going to be home, mom?" he asks.

"I don't know," I say. "I'm going to go in the Legion and have a couple of beers and then I'll be home." "OK, mom. I love you. See you later," he says.

"Yep. Love ya. Bye," I say.

Now I'm wondering what the hell Shelley is doing at my house, alone with my husband, when she told me that she was going to meet me at volleyball. I am so mad that there is no way that I can go home right now. I head into the Legion and order a beer. My mind is racing. Anxiety is building inside me. The thought of overreacting scares the hell out of me. Of course it's not really something that I want to talk about with my "summer friends." I sit quietly and drink my beer, thinking about what I'm going to do when I get home. The room is loud, people are talking, and the jukebox is on. All I feel is numb.

When I leave, I debate about texting Brian, to warn him that I'm on my way. I don't really want to come home to my husband fucking Shelley bent over the deck or something. I decide to let it be. Trying to remind myself it's probably nothing, I drive faster. About a quarter mile from home, I turn off my headlights. When I pull into the driveway, the outside light is on out on the deck. I can see people sitting at the patio table but they are nothing more than figures. I'm not sure what's worse, finding your husband fucking your friend or wondering if he already did. I move into the entryway. I can hear voices. I don't even want to see either of them. I fly down the stairs, worried about the kids, trying to protect them from whatever the hell has been going on. The boys are watching TV.

"Hey guys," I say. "What's going on?" They both turn around and look at me.

"Just watching TV," Bryce says. "How was volleyball, Mom?" "Pretty good," I lie. All I can think about is the little bitch upstairs with my husband. "Where's your Dad?"

I hear voices in the living room. They must have figured out that I was home. I suppose they are feeling a little busted.

"Hey Erika," Shelley hollers down the stairs.

"Hey," I say, giving her the cold shoulder.

"How was volleyball," she yells again.

"Fine," I lie again, with the colder shoulder. Brian chimes in, "Are you going to come upstairs?" Great, now we have a threesome.

"No, I'm good," I say. Bryce is watching me, probably hoping that we're not going to fight.

Shelley shouts down the staircase, "Well, I'm going to head out," she says.

"OK, see you later," I mutter under my breath, "Good riddance." A few minutes later, Brian comes downstairs.

"What are you doing, Erika?" he asks.

"Nothing, just checking on the kids," I say. "What was Shelley doing here?"

"Nothing," he responds with irritation. "We were just talking. She called and asked if I had anything going on and I told her that you were at volleyball and I was just hanging out having some beers."

"Yeah, whatever. She already knew that I had volleyball. She was supposed to meet me there, remember? But she decided to come out here and be alone with you and you told her it was fine. Really, Brian?

Do you really think that's ok?" I ask.

"Why in the hell did you come in the driveway with the lights off?" he asks.

"Well, I was kind of wondering what the hell you two were doing out on the deck alone?" I ask.

"We were just talking," he says. "Becca was out there the whole time."

"Yeah, good, because she's 3 and she would really know what the hell is going on," I say sarcastically.

"Whatever," he says.

"Bryce called me earlier to tell me that Shelley was here," I tell him.

"Why?" he asks.

"I don't know," I say. "Apparently he was worried about what was going on here."

"Nothing was going on, Erika," he says.

I immediately don't believe him.

"OK, well," I say, "But I don't really know why Shelley would come out here without me being here?"

"How should I know?" he asks.

"Why didn't you tell her no?" I ask.

"Why should I? We were just talking. You're blowing this all out of proportion," he says.

"Whatever," I say. "That's bullshit. I bet you wouldn't like it if I did the same thing with Cole some night."

"I wouldn't care," he says. "You're totally overreacting about this.

You made Shelley feel like shit when you said nothing to her at all."

"Tough," I said. "I don't really care."

I walk away. I am too damn mad to even talk to him anymore. How in the hell can he be mad at me when she shouldn't have even been at our house in the first place? What an asshole. All of a sudden, I feel like someone is watching us through the dining room window. When I look over, something moves outside. It's probably just a bird or an animal, but I want to know so I decide to go look. I go out the patio door off the kitchen and stand and look out over the railing at the pool. There is nothing there. Then I walk around the deck on the front of the house, heading for the chairs on the front porch. In the space between the deck and the concrete, I step on something sharp that makes me wince. Dammit. I look down and there is a piece of glass on the concrete. I cut my foot. It is bleeding all over. I hobble inside, trying not to get blood all over the place.

I holler for Brian to come help me. When he comes out to the living room, he is irritated.

"What did you go outside for in the first place?" he asks. "I

wanted to get some air. I was just walking around," I tell him. My toe bleeds on and off all night long. For some reason, it feels

like an omen. I decide to sleep on the couch. I hardly sleep. Little did I know that night is the start of many more nights on the couch. And I have the worst summer of my life ahead of me.

Chapter 7

*T*he next morning when I get up, Brian and I make a point of not speaking to each other. He grunts a goodbye to me as I leave but says nothing more. When I get to work, all I can think about is last night. I feel like I overreacted, probably made something out of nothing. I really didn't want to do that to a friend I just met. I mean, really, Shelley hasn't really done anything too terribly wrong. Yes, she was alone with my husband and yes, she didn't come to volleyball, but she also may have just changed her mind. The Girl Scout in me feels like I need to give her the benefit of the doubt. When I get to my desk in the morning, I sit down and start an e-mail to her.

To: Shelley

From: Erika

Date: Thursday, July 31, 2007 7:35 a.m.

Subject: Last Night

Hey, Shelley. I just wanted to apologize for what happened last night. I think I overreacted when I found out that you were at our house when you told me that you were going to meet me at volleyball. Brian and I have had a lot of issues with trust and I'm sorry that I put you in the middle of that. I hope that we can still be friends. Maybe we can get together this weekend with the kids and just hang out by the pool or something. Hopefully you can accept my apology. Talk to you soon.

-Erika

Almost as soon as I send it, I get a reply back from her.

To: Erika

From: Shelley

Date: Thursday, July 31, 2007 7:52 a.m.

Subject: Re: Last Night

Hey, Erika! No problem. I could tell something was wrong when you didn't come upstairs when I was leaving, but I figured it was just something between you and Brian. Cole and I have had our own ups and downs so I understand what you mean. No hard feelings. This weekend sounds great! Maybe Saturday afternoon we could come over. Cole is going to be working all day but the boys and I could come over and he could meet us later. Let me know what time works for you guys.

Thanks!

-Shelley

We chat back and forth by e-mail a couple more times, trying to smooth things over. I am hoping that I can get over the whole situation quickly. When I get home later, I tell Brian about my e-mail to Shelley. I'm not really surprised when he says nothing at all. That seems to be the typical response from him these days.

That Saturday, Shelley comes over with the boys to hang out with us. Reid fell asleep on the car ride to our house so we lay him down in our portable crib in the basement. The rest of us head out to the pool. I put together a tray of cheese and meat and crackers and cut up some fruit for the kids to have while they are swimming. Brian is out in the garden.

"So how was your week at work?" Shelley asks.

"Oh, pretty good," I say, except that there was something more that happened this week. For a moment, I can't really even recall what it is. Then I remember the night of volleyball. It is the woman sitting across from me trying to get a little closer to my husband. And now I'm entertaining her by our pool. "How 'bout you?"

"Oh, fine, you know, dirty diapers and dirty faces, cooking and naps and that good stuff. Cole worked every day until dark so I was home with the kids pretty much all day, every day. It just starts to wear on me after awhile," she says.

"What do you mean, the kids or the daycare or what?" I ask. "No, I love doing daycare because then I get to spend time with the boys while they are growing up. But I miss seeing Cole when he is working all day. By the time he gets home, the kids are already in bed and he hasn't seen them all day, and I'm tired and just feel like going to bed by then," she complains.

"Oh, I see what you mean. You kind of work different shifts in a way, so you don't get a lot of time together. I guess I'm lucky that way. Brian and I work pretty much the same schedule. Sometimes he has to work a little bit longer at times, and he works a lot from home, but he's still here with us, so that's good I guess," I say. "And he has to travel for work, but sometimes it's nice for him to be gone for a little while. I travel too."

"Yeah, well Cole just works because he always thinks we need the extra money, and we're fine. I keep telling him that we don't need the money, but he keeps taking side jobs after he's done at his regular job," she whines.

"I get it. I think it's just a man thing. They just want to provide for their families. It amazes me all the time how men are just born that way," I tell her. "They just want to make a better life for their family than the one that they had. And sometimes when they're doing that, they forget about all of the important stuff that their missing. Meals and books and bedtime, concerts, church, the stuff that matters."

I don't want to sound condescending to her, like I have so much experience in the ways of the world. I've been with the same man all my life, but so many men that I've talked to just want to be the provider. It just really matters to them. And yet, women want to make their own money, feel empowered, able to live without a man if they have to.

"Yeah, that sounds exactly like him," she says. "He misses so much. He just doesn't even realize that it matters to me," she says. "It matters to the boys."

Cory gets out of the pool, crying and rubbing his eyes. He got hit in the face by a football thrown by one of my older boys. Shelley grabs a towel, wraps it around him tightly, and pulls him in close to her. For a few minutes, she's snuggling with him. Then, as quickly as he came over, he was gone, back on his way into the pool.

Then, I say, "Well, men and women are just different that way, I guess. Just remember, Cole's just trying to do what's best for your family. He wants to provide for you."

She looks at me, shaking her head, then says, "I know, you're right. I just don't understand why he always thinks we need to make more and more money."

"You know," I say, "You need to tell him, tell him how you feel. Right now you're both moving in different directions in what you want in life, and until you tell him what you want, you're going to keep doing that."

"Yeah, you're probably right," she says, getting up to go check on Reid.

I know I am, but I leave it at that, because then I start wondering if I even know the direction that my own marriage is headed these days. The kids swim for a little bit longer but they are starting to get hungry. Brian comes over from the garden with handfuls of vegetables. Cole is supposed to join us later for dinner, but Shelley gets a call around 4:30 from him. He tells her that he's going to have to work later than he expected and that we should eat without him.

Shelley stands after she hangs up.

"OK, well since Cole's not going to make it, I'm just going to head home with the boys. I'm going to have to do baths and bedtime by myself when I get there," she says, sounding discouraged. "Thanks for having us over today."

"Oh sure, this was fun," I say, walking her toward the stairs. "Hopefully the boys are tired and will sleep well tonight. See you soon."

Then, Brian comes over by me and we watch Shelley walk up the stairs with Reid in her arms and Cory trailing behind her, not wanting to go home. I realize it's been a while since I've had a baby in my arms. Boy, am I glad that phase of my life is over.

Chapter 8

I don't talk to Shelley for a few weeks after that, which is fine with me because I feel like I need to slow down our friendship and get to know her better. I get a text from her the Thursday before the big summer festival in town wondering if we are going to the dance that Friday night. Summer festivals and street dances are a big deal in the boondocks. Some of us joke that it should really be on our list of national holidays because we all have to take the following Monday off to recover. There is stuff going on all weekend, but we usually go to the dance on Friday, stay home on Saturday, then to the parade on

Sunday. We have our routine, and I don't want to break it. I tell her that I'm not sure, only if we can find someone to watch the kids. I secretly hope that they can't find a sitter or that my answer is enough to get her to stay home. I don't want any more drama with them, and I am trying my best to be diplomatic without coming across as a complete bitch. I am starting to get the feeling that Shelley is one of those women who will do whatever it takes to get what she wants. Unfortunately, what she wants just might happen to be my husband. But I have no reason to not trust Brian, and I certainly don't want her to scare me into staying home just because she is going to be there.

On Friday I take the day off to spend it with the kids. Mid-afternoon, I get another text from Shelley wondering if we are going to the dance. I want to lie, but I can't. I tell her that we are, but we won't be there until later. Brian gets home from work around 5 and we have dinner with the kids. Then I get ready to go out while Brian hangs out with the kids. I decide to wear something a little sexier. When I walk into the living room, Brian turns his head from the newspaper.

"Wow, lookin' good," he winks and smiles.

"Thanks," I say.

After we take the kids to his parents' house, we head back to town and stop at the bar for a drink. After a couple of beers, we decide to leave our car there and walk uptown where the street dance is going on. About a block from the dance, Brian is barraged by someone from behind. He almost knocks me over, and as I turn around I see Shelley has jumped on his back. I give him an unsympathetic look and roll my eyes and keep walking ahead of them. The three of them stay together. When I get to the door, I pay for myself and walk in, not wanting to be anywhere near them. I get a drink and find some friends to chat with, but don't say anything about what just happened until I run into my cousin Alicia.

"You'll never believe what happened when we walked in," I say, then telling her the story.

"I'm sure," she says as rolls her eyes. "What the fuck is she thinking?"

"I have no idea, but nothing like being subtle, right?" I say. "Wow, that takes balls," she says.

"I know. And if she doesn't stay away from him I'm going to kick her ass," I say. That is so not like me to say that.

"I'm with you," she says, winking. "I've got your back." That's so not like her either.

Alicia grabs my hand and we head out to the dance floor. I keep looking for Brian but I can't see him anywhere outside. Finally I decide to go into the bar to see if he is in there. When I get inside, I see Cole and Shelley and Brian standing together by the pool table. I head the other way toward the bar. I really just want to go home, but I don't want Shelley to change my plans just because she is flirting with my husband. I get a drink from the bar, and on my way back outside I notice that Brian and Shelley are gone. Cole is still standing there watching his friends play pool so I make my way through the crowd to say hello.

"How's it goin'?" I ask.

"Alright," he says.

"So where did those two go?" I ask.

"What two?" he asks back pretending like he doesn't know who I am talking about.

"Your wife and my husband," I reply.

"Out to dance I guess," he says.

"You're kidding me," I say.

"No, why?" he replies.

"Don't you think it's a little strange that your wife and my husband are out there dancing without us?" I ask him.

"No," he says. "I don't really think it's that big of deal." "Well, I think it's a little weird," I say.

I look across the room, not really sure how to say what I want to. "I think there's something going on with those two, Cole," I warn him.

"What do you mean something? Like what?" he asks.

"I don't know," I say. "Either they've already had sex or they're going to, but there is definitely something going on." "I don't think so," he says.

"Well, I do. And I'm sorry that you don't want to believe it, but there's just too much weird stuff going on that doesn't make sense," I tell him.

I walk away, tears in my eyes and a little bit of fear of what I will find when I get outside. And then, as I walk off the back step of the bar, there they are, out on the dance floor. Every part of me wants to go out there and punch her in the face. But yet, he is right there too, holding her close for little moments and twisting her around. I don't even remember which song it was, but I'm glad because I would probably just hate it anyway. I walk straight over to them and tell Brian that it is time to go home.

"It's only 12:30," he says.

"I don't care. We're both drunk and it's time to go," I demand. I walk away, praying like hell he will follow me. I do not want to make a big scene, but I suppose I probably already have. When I get to the entrance, I turn around, and there he is. Honestly, I can't believe it. I did not expect him to follow me. I just know it is time to go home where we can fight in private.

"What in the hell is the matter with you?" he says. "It's just a dance."

"Whatever, just a dance," I say. "Shelley jumped on your back when we got here like she was your girlfriend, you were nowhere to be found all night, and then I finally find you out on the dance floor with her."

"Big deal," he says. "You're making something out of nothing." "I don't like it, Brian," I say. "I don't know what else to say. I'm your wife and I don't like it. Doesn't that mean anything to you?" Of course, I'm crying now, and tears are streaming down my face, along with all of my mascara.

"What do you want me to say?" he asks.

"Nothing," I tell him. "There's nothing more to say about it. I just want to go home."

And then we do.

The next day, it is raining when I wake up. It is one of those kinds of rains that feels like it can go on for days. It's slow and wet and even. Brian goes to get the kids from his parents' house in the morning, but otherwise, we stay home all day and hang out with the kids. By Saturday night, we are all exhausted from the weather. There are flash flood warnings everywhere. I am glad we are spending the evening at home. The only thing that would make it better is if I felt like Brian wanted to be there with us.

"What are you doing?" I ask, watching him texting on his phone. "Nothing, just texting someone," he says.

"Who?" I ask.

He looks at me annoyed, as if I'm not his wife and it's none of my business.

"It's Shelley," he says. "She's wondering if we're going out tonight."

"Tell her it's none of her damn business what we're doing," I say quickly. "Why in the hell is she texting you and not me anyway?" "How should I know?" he asks.

God dammit, if I could patent that answer for him I would be a billionaire by now.

"Well, what did you say?" I ask.

"I told her I didn't know," he says.

Well, no wonder I feel like he doesn't want to be home with us. "Why would you say that if you know we're staying home?" I ask. "Well, I didn't know if we would maybe go out later," he says. "Don't you wanna stay home?" I ask.

"I don't know," he says.

"Well, you go ahead and go out if you want to, but I'm staying home," I tell him.

"No, I'm not going out then," he says, looking irritated. "Settle down."

I turn away and realize that Bryce is watching us. We're not really fighting but I'd like to be. I'm wondering why the hell she is texting him, and not really sure what I'm going to do to stop it. I can ask her to stop. Brian can ask her to stop. We can block her number on our phones. But in the end, I know that there is nothing that I can do to stop it from happening. If they want each other badly enough and the chemistry is there, then there is no stopping the inevitable. In a way, I feel like he's already gone somehow. Like there is something happening that is out of my control. Like they've already gone too far.

Brian changes the channel. Katy Perry is singing 'Waking up in Vegas,' which somehow seems appropriate for the moment. Soon, there is a musician named Ferras who joins her on stage to sing a song I've never heard before, called 'Rush.'

It's a rush I can't explain,

Like you shot something crazy into my brain.

And I'm ten feet off the ground, And I don't, want to come back down.

Beautiful lyrics. I'm a little sad wondering how I got to be 33-years-old and have never experienced that kind of love in my life.

As I look over at Brian, I wonder if I ever will.

Chapter 9

*T*he next day we're up early getting ready to go to my grandparents for their annual chicken dinner, provided by the American Legion. After that, we head to the parade and stay for a while afterwards to dance and drink beer and let the kids play at the park. The band is fantastic. They are playing old country classics and a little bit of rock and roll. Becca is bobbing up and down, making a show for the crowd. I sweep her up in my arms and take her to the dance floor when the band starts playing Van Morrison's Brown Eyed Girl. She's mine forever. We twist and turn, and she's giggling and laughing. At the end of the song, I look over and Brian is watching us. He smiles back at me as the song ends. Becca and I leave the dance floor. It starts to rain again. Either time to go home, or head to the bar. Brian asks me what I want to do, and we have our usual banter back and forth because neither of us wants to make the decision.

"Well, let's see if your parents can watch the kids," I say. "If not, then we'll just go home."

"Sounds good," he says as walks away to call them.

"They're on their way right now," he says as he walks back toward me. "We better go find the boys."

Brian heads over to the park, passing Shelley on his way there. I wonder for a moment if they exchanged glances, but warn myself to put it out of my mind. I don't want to ruin a good night. We kiss the kids goodbye and send them off with Brian's parents, then we head uptown.

Within minutes, Cole and Shelley walk in. From across the bar, I watch as Shelley approaches Brian with a smile. I turn the other way toward the dance floor, not wanting to make something out of nothing. I figure I can probably get his attention with a little dirty dancing, or at least enjoy myself in the process. Brian sits down at the table closest to the dance floor. He is facing me, watching me for a moment, but then Shelley and Cole approach the table. Shelley sits next to Brian, and Cole sits across from him. There are 4 or 5 others sitting there too. Perfect, I can see everything that goes on and I'm certain he won't misbehave. Of course then I realize it's not just him I have to worry about. Shelley puts her hands under the table. I'm close enough that I can see when she moves her hands but far enough away to not see what the hell she is doing with them. I turn my back to them and pretend to not notice. That's all she probably really wants is a little attention anyway. I figure I can just ignore them. I check the clock. It's already 12:30. Next thing I know they are both standing up and heading for the door. Cole and I are watching them. I have no idea what she is up to now, but I don't like it. I walk over to the table by Cole.

"Where are those two going?" I ask him.

"Out to have a smoke," Cole says.

"What the hell," I say, "Brian doesn't smoke." "He said he needed some air," he says.

Yeah, I'll bet.

"Well, I'm not really comfortable with those two being alone together," I say.

He looks at me strangely, eyebrows bent and his head tilted sideways.

"Nothing is going on, Erika," he says. "Trust me." "Whatever," I say.

He's pissed off at me now. He stands up and walks over to the door, pushing it open in a furry. Good, I think. Now at least they won't be alone together. I figure it's time to go home. I know that neither of us can drive. We've been drinking all afternoon and the last thing we need is for one of us to get a DUI or kill someone. I call my Dad for a ride. He says he'll be there in a few minutes. He wants me to wait at the door. Like hell, I think. I'm not going anywhere near that bitch. The DJ announces the last slow song of the evening, Fergie's "Big Girls Don't Cry," another omen. Our old friend Dave asks me to dance. I've known Dave most of my life, so I say yes, and we head to the dance floor. In a moment, Brian is followed into the bar by Shelley and Cole. Brian and Shelley make their way to the dance floor. I'm certain it's retaliation for me dancing with Dave. I shoot Brian a look across the floor and of course he turns the other way. I'm furious but smile anyway and chat with Dave as the song ends. When it's over, I give him a kiss on the cheek and head over toward Brian.

"My Dad is on his way to get us. He'll be here any minute," I tell him.

"Why?" he asks.

"Well, I can't drive, and I'm pretty sure that you can't either," I tell him.

"Well, I'm not ready to go home yet," he says.

"It's 12:30, Brian, and we've been drinking all day. It's time to go home," I tell him.

"No, I want to stay," he says, almost demanding now. I don't feel like arguing with him. I'm ready to go home. I'm his wife and I don't feel like I should have to beg him to go home with me. "How are you going to get home then?" I ask.

He looks over at the table.

"Dave will give me a ride, or Cole and Shelley can," he suggests. "Fine, whatever," I say.

I head toward the door and see my Dad waving a hand that it's time to go. I follow my brother out the door on the way. When I get outside, Shelley is out there smoking again, watching me get into the car. I want to flip her off but decide to be a grown-up.

"Where is Brian?" my Dad asks.

"He's going to get a ride from Cole and Shelley," I tell him. I look out the window as Cole and Brian walk out of the bar together. The three of them start walking up the street in the same direction that we are headed. She has a smug little grin on her face like she beat me in a game. I'd like to slap it off her face.

"Why isn't he going home with you," he asks, "His wife?" "I don't know," I say. "You'd have to ask him that question." My brother chimes in, in a slur, "Just leave him then. Let him get his own ride home."

Dad shakes his head and puts the car into drive. We reach the corner before turning on Broadway, and the three of them are standing together, watching us drive by. I look at him in disbelief. Dad keeps driving. When we are almost out of town, he stops the car.

"Do you want me to go back and ask him if he wants a ride home," he asks.

"It's up to you. I already asked him and he said he was going to get a ride from Dave, or Cole and Shelley," I say.

"Well, what the hell is going on that he wouldn't go home with his own wife?" my Dad says, disgusted.

"I have no idea," I say. "I have no idea what the hell is going on." My Dad turns the car around and heads back to the bar. When we get there, neither Cole or Shelley or Brian is anywhere outside. He double-parks out front and heads back into the bar. A few minutes later, my Dad comes out of the bar, followed by Brian. I have no idea what he said to Brian. In that moment, I don't know if I am more relieved that he is coming home with me, or just glad that he isn't going somewhere with Shelley.

Chapter 10

*I*was quiet all the way home. Tears are welling in my eyes, and I know that if I say one word I will be bawling. My lip is even quivering. My Dad and brother and Brian fill the car with idle chitchat, talking about the rain and the water and the storm. I just want to tell them to shut up. As we pull into the driveway, I thank Dad for the ride. Brian mumbles something in his drunkenness, and I want to backhand him across the head. When we get inside the house, I can't handle it in any longer.

"What are you thinking," I say. "You would seriously stay there with them instead of going home with your wife? How could you do that?"

"I don't know," he says.

"What do you mean, you don't know," I holler. "Really? Am I that awful to live with?"

"I just didn't want to go home because I knew this is how you were going to be," he says.

"Well, damn right I was," I shoot back. "You sat next to Shelley all night and every time I looked, she was staring at you.

"So what," he says.

"I was watching her when she had her hand on your leg under the table," I tell him.

"She did not," he objects.

"Bullshit," I throw back. "Yes, she did. Why do you always fucking lie about shit?

"I'm not lying," he says again.

"Whatever," I say. "And then you dance with her? Why in the hell would you dance with her when you already know that I'm feeling insecure?"

"It's just a dance. And you were dancing with Dave anyway. No big deal," he says.

"We've known Dave forever. We've known Shelley for 3 months. It matters to me. After Friday night, I would think you would know that. I'm starting to wonder if you even want to be with me anymore," I admit.

He just looks at me.

"You have nothing to say to that? What in the hell is going on with you?" I ask.

"I don't know," he says again.

"Do you even want to be with me anymore?" I ask.

"I don't know," he finally admits.

"What? Are you kidding me?" I say.

Silence again. The first tear rolls down my face.

"Oh my God, Brian," I say. "We've been married for almost 11 years and you don't know if you want to be with me?" "I'm just confused right now," he says.

"What do you mean, you're confused. About what?" I

ask. "I don't know," he says.

"What is going on with you and Shelley?" I ask.

Silence.

"What, Brian? Just say it." I say.

"I have feelings for her," he says.

My heart sinks. I don't know how this unraveled so fast. I don't know what to do or what to say. The anger inside me is building and I'm trying to suppress it like I always do. Save it for a rainy day.

"What the fuck? Are you kidding me? Are you in love with her?" I ask.

"I don't know," he says.

"You have feelings for her? That's fucking great. So where do I fit into all of this?" I ask.

"I don't know," he says.

"Do you want to be with her or what?" I ask.

"I don't know," he says again.

One more of those and I'm going to kick him in the balls. "Jesus Christ. Do you know anything?" I ask. "I'm just really confused right now," he says.

"What am I going to tell the kids? That their Dad is in love with someone else?" I ask.

"I never said I was in love with her," finally coming back with an answer. Praise God.

I walk to the window, cross my arms and try to fight back more tears.

"Well, maybe you should figure out what you want. I don't want to be in this marriage alone," I tell him.

I look at Brian and look away. I can't even believe we are having this conversation. He gets up from the couch and starts walking away. "Where are you going?" I ask.

"To bed," he says.

As he's walking away, I want to throw my phone at him. Then, in a moment, it's flying out of my hand and headed straight at him. What a son of a bitch. It hits him on the back.

"What the hell are you doing?" he asks.

I don't even respond. I just walk over and start picking up the pieces of my phone. Anxiety comes over like me like a wave. I am angry. I am sad. I think about all of the little moments that got us to this point. Good grief, memories of our wedding, our kids being born, building houses, vacations, and the bad stuff too. I just want to leave, but I can't drive anywhere. I know I've had too much to drink. I decide to call Janet.

"Hello," she says, just waking.

"Janet, it's Erika," I say.

"Is everything OK? What's going on?" she asks, panic in her voice. "I need you to come get me," I tell her.

"Why?" she asks.

"I'm here with Brian and he just told me that he doesn't know if he wants to be married to me anymore," I say.

"What?" she asks. "What is going on?"

"It's a long story. I need to get out of this house right now. I don't want to be alone with him. Can you come get me and just go for a drive?" I ask.

"Sure, I'll be over in a bit," she says.

Fifteen minutes feels like hours when you're drunk. I sit in the living room, relentlessly watching the road for her car. Finally I see headlights and she pulls in the driveway. When I get to the car, her face is tired, groggy. I feel badly that I got her out of bed. I should have just gone for a walk. I should have tried to sleep on it.

"What is going on?" she asks.

I tell her about our night, everything, even things I never said to Brian. I share little moments that I caught between the two of them. She has known my husband all her life and she can't believe this is happening. We drive the back roads. Down in the valleys, to town, even the cemetery where Brian's sister is buried. We drive for an hour and just talk. I have never had a friend that I could trust to talk to about something like this. She is everything to me.

We head toward home. As we approach the field drive to our house, I see a car in the driveway. At first, I can't tell whose it is, but then it starts backing up. I realize it is Shelley's car. She is at our house, alone with him. Janet pulls into the field drive.

"Whose car is that?" she says?

"Whose do you think," I say.

"What is she doing here?" she says, assuming the

answer. "I have no idea," I say.

The car tears down the driveway building dust and is coming straight at us. Soon, the headlights of the two cars meet. I look at the driver's seat and see the blond hair and I know it is Shelley. There is someone in the passenger seat next to her, but I can't see who it is.

It's really dark inside the car.

Janet says, "It's her."

"Well, who was in the passenger seat," I ask.

"Brian," she says.

Before I even turn around, the car has left the driveway and is headed west on the highway toward town. I can't believe this is happening. As I'm getting out of the car, she asks me what I am going to do. I wonder, does she mean right now or in the next hour or tomorrow or the next day. My thoughts and heart are racing. I can't get my head around any of this.

"I don't know. It makes me sick," I say.

"Me too. I have known Brian all my life and this just doesn't seem like him," she says.

"It wasn't him in that car. I don't think it was him. It really didn't look like him. He's probably hiding out somewhere because he's embarrassed about all of this," I tell her, actually believing what I am saying at the very moment.

Janet looks at me in disbelief. When we get in the house, I start yelling for him, like he's a dog who won't come home. I take off through the house, leaving Janet behind in the living room. Frantically, I look everywhere. I look in the kids' bedrooms, under their beds and in their closets; in our bedroom and the bathroom shower; the kitchen and living room; the guest suite in the basement; the other bathroom; the garage. In desperation, I even go the shed, turn on the lights and holler his name.

"He's not here, Erika," Janet says. "I told you, he was in the car." "What am I going to do?" I ask.

"I don't know," she says. "Do you want me to stay with you?" "I don't know. I don't really want to be alone right now," I admit. "Well, how 'bout if I stay with you until I have to get up for work," she tells me.

I look at the clock. It's already 2:20. I can't believe it. I look at her, tears in my eyes. I walk over to the loveseat to sit down. In a panic, I decide to call Brian, not just once, but over and over again. I have no idea how many times I call him, but he doesn't answer. Desperately, I decide to call Cole and Shelley's house, to see if he went there with her. A woman's voice answers, but it isn't Shelley.

"Hello?" the woman says.

"Hi, this is Erika Daniels calling," I say." Is Cole there?" "Yes, but he's sleeping," she says.

"Well, I'm a friend of Cole and Shelley's, and my husband is out driving around somewhere with Shelley and I wondered if Cole knows where they might be? Can you please wake him up for me?" I ask.

"No, I'm not going to wake him up," she says, her soft voice immediately hardening.

"So you're telling me that I'm calling his house and asking for him, and you're not going to wake him up?" I confirm.

"No, I'm not going to wake him up," she says again, like I didn't hear it the first time.

"You've got to be kidding me," I say.

"No, I'm not kidding you," she says. "Good night."

And then she hangs up on me. Janet is watching all of this in disbelief. I decide to call Brian's mom. If anybody can get him to answer the phone, it's her.

"Nnn, hello," she says in a sleepy voice.

"It's Erika," I tell her.

"Hi, Erika," she says.

"I'm calling because I wondered if you would call Brian and make sure he's alright," I say.

"Well, where is he?" she asks.

"I don't know for sure. I think he left here with Shelley. I've been calling his cell phone but he won't answer when I call and I'm worried about him. I just want to make sure he's alright," she says. "Well, what is he doing with Shelley?" she asks.

"I don't know what he's doing with her, but he left here with her. I was on a drive with Janet and when we came back they were leaving here together," I tell her.

There is a long pause. I don't know what else to say to her so I wait for her reply.

"Well, you know, none of this would have happened if you hadn't gotten to be friends with that girl to begin with," she says, a sting in her voice.

I'm speechless, but only for a moment.

"Are you kidding me?" I screech into the phone. "You think this is my fault?"

"Please don't yell at me," she says. "What do you want me to do?" "I just wanted to know if you will call him to see if he will answer his phone, and make sure he is ok," I say.

"Alright, I will," she says.

"And can you call me back after you talk to him so I know he's ok?" I ask.

"No, I'm not going to call you back," she says.

"OK, well, can you please just call him then?" I ask.

OK, I will," she says, and hangs up, abruptly.

I'm still standing there holding the phone to my ear. I look at Janet and her mouth is hanging wide open.

"Did she just say that it was your fault that Brian left with her?" she asks.

"Yes, she did. Unbelievable, what the fuck?" I say.

"I'm sorry, Erika. I don't know what's going on," she says. "Don't be sorry. It's not your fault. Let's just get some sleep. You have to get up and work in the morning," she says.

Janet is on the sofa and I'm lying on the loveseat. At first I can't sleep, hoping that any minute a car will pull in the driveway and Brian will be home. I must have dozed off because the next thing I know I wake up to Janet's cell phone alarm going off.

Chapter 11

I open my eyes and Janet is already standing up putting her shoes on. I get up from the couch and go to walk her out to her car.

"So he must not have come home then, huh?" Janet asks. "I guess not," I say.

"What are you going to do?" she asks.

"I have no idea," I tell her.

"Well, call me if you need anything," she says as she leans in to give me a big hug. I try hard not to cry.

"I will," I say, as I open the door. I follow her out to the front porch. I wave as she's walking away.

I shut the door and turn around. Within seconds, someone is knocking on the front door. I peer through the sidelight. It's Janet.

"He's sitting in his truck," she tells me.

"What do you mean?" I ask, shocked.

"I went to get into my car and saw him sitting in the passenger seat of his truck," she says.

"What the hell," I say. "What is he doing in there?"

We head outside to take a look. As I walk around the corner of the house, I see Brian sitting in the passenger seat of his pick-up. As I get closer, I can see that he is sleeping. I open the door. His pants are unzipped and his hands are resting over his zipper.

"Brian!" I shout, startling him awake. "What the hell is going on?" He slurs his usual, "Nothing."

"What do you mean nothing?" I scream. "You're passed out in the passenger seat of your truck with your zipper down." He sits there, then looks down at his zipper, and up at me. Janet starts walking away.

"I'll let you two be alone," she says.

I walk away from Brian and follow Janet. I hug her again.

"Thanks for everything," I say. "I really do appreciate it." "You're welcome," she says. "That's what friends are for. Call me, ok?" "Yeah," I say, knowing that I probably won't. I'm going to want to forget about this night as quickly as I can.

As she pulls out of the driveway, I look back at Brian in disgust and head back to the house. A few minutes later, the garage door starts opening and he walks in through the mudroom door. He heads straight toward our bedroom, like a teenager trying to avoid a run-in with his parents. I follow him and we meet in the hallway.

"What in the hell happened to you last night?" I ask.

"Nothing," he says.

"What do you mean, nothing? You left here with Shelley at 2 in the morning and God only knows what time you got home because you didn't have the balls to come in the house. Where were you?" I ask.

"We went for a drive, all over the place. Then we went to the State Park and just sat there and talked," he says.

"And you expect me to believe that?" I ask.

"No, why would you, Erika, you never believe anything I say. Why would you believe me now?" he throws back.

"Oh my God," I say. "Now you're going to turn this around on me, like I'm the bad person?"

"No, I'm not," he says. "I'm just saying that you never believe me anyway, no matter what I say."

"Well, how about if you start with the truth?" I ask.

"That is the truth," he says.

"So what else happened?" I ask.

"Nothing," he says. "I'm done talking about this."

"Oh ok, you tell me you have feelings for this girl, then you stay out all night with her, and now you say we're just supposed to be done talking about it?" I ask.

"Yep, that's it. I'm done. I don't have to explain myself to you or anyone else," he says as he walks toward the kitchen. I go to our bedroom.

Wow. I guess sometimes there is just nothing left to say. And we probably both need a timeout anyway.

Chapter 12

A couple of hours later, Brian comes into the bedroom and starts getting dressed.

"Where are you going?" I ask.

"I need to go for a drive," he says.

"Where?" I ask.

"Just a drive," he says. "To clear my head."

"Are you going somewhere with Shelley or what? If we're going to try to make this work you're not going to be able to see her anymore," I warn him.

"She wants to talk," he says.

"About what? If you didn't have sex with her then there's nothing to talk about, right? What do you possibly have to talk to her about?" I ask.

I'm yelling now. I don't really know how to be angry without yelling. In fact, I'm not even sure that it's possible.

"She just wants to talk," he says again.

"Fine, go. Be with her, Brian," I tell him. "If that's what you want, then just do it."

He walks out of the bedroom. I want to run after him and push him or throw something at him, but I don't even have the energy anymore. I feel like there is nothing I can do to fight it. He stated it so matter of factly. This is what I am doing and you have no choice but to accept it. I guess it's the truth. I have to make my own choices. I decide at that very moment that when he gets home from doing whatever the hell it is he is doing with Shelley that I am going to ask him to move out.

When he isn't home an hour later, I call his cell phone. He doesn't answer. How reassuring. I suppose that they are just having an adult conversation about the fantastic sex that they had last night. I call again a few minutes later. No answer. Finally, he picks up on the third try.

"Whattya' want," he says.

"Where are you?" I say.

"I told you, I'm on a drive," he says.

"With Shelley," I say, assuming the worst.

"Yes, Erika, I already told you I was going with Shelley," he says. My heart starts to ache but somehow I'm relieved because he told me the truth.

"When are you coming home?" I ask.

"I'll be home in 15 or 20 minutes, and then I'm going to get the kids," he says.

"OK," I say. "See you when you get here."

When I hang up the phone, I am sobbing. It feels like my world is slipping out from under me. It's out of control and spinning fast. My body is full of fear that reminds me of my first panic attack so many years before. Then I sleep.

I wake to the sound of the shower running. I have no idea how long I have been sleeping but I feel refreshed. For a moment, I forget that I just had the worst night of my life. Then I realize that it is probably Brian who has the shower running. He must have come home while I was sleeping. If there is any chance that I am ever going to know if he slept with Shelley the night before, it is now.

I get out of bed to go to the bathroom. The door to the bathroom is shut. That's strange. He always leaves the door open when he showers. As I open the door to the bathroom, he turns from the sink and moves quickly into the shower. I pause for a moment, thinking that I should stop, but I can't. I have to do it now or I will never know the truth.

I push open the door to the shower, and peer in.

"I have to ask you something," I say.

"What?" he replies, irritation in his voice. I pause again. I don't know how to say it.

"I want to smell you," I say.

"What do you mean?" he asks.

"I want to smell your junk" I say, looking directly at it. "Why" he says, grabbing for the soap.

"Don't" I say, almost begging him to stop.

"Don't what?" he asks.

"Wash yourself," I tell him.

"Why?" he asks.

"Because if you wash yourself I'll never know if you had sex with her," I admit the theory behind my plan.

"What do you mean?" he asks.

"If you let me smell you, if you had sex with Shelley then her smell will be all over you, right?" I ask.

He says nothing. He just looks at me with strange eyes, like I'm out of my mind. I guess by this time I probably am.

"So, will you let me?" I beg. Tears are welling in my eyes now. "No, Erika. I am not going to let you smell me. Get out of here," he demands.

"Are you kidding me? I am your wife," I say. "You'll let me suck your cock all the time but you won't let me smell you? What if this is the only way that you can prove to me that you aren't lying, that you didn't fuck her last night?"

"Tough, I'm not doing it," he says. "Leave."

In disbelief, I turn and walk out of the bathroom. The one chance that he has to prove all of my suspicions are wrong and he won't even do it. There is only one thing that I want to do. I crawl back into bed and pull the covers up over my head.

When he comes out of the shower, I pretend to be sleeping. I want to be, so that should at least count for something. He gets dressed, and as he walks toward the bedroom door I sit up and ask him if he wants to talk about anything.

"What is there to talk about?" he asks.

"I want you to move out," I tell him.

"No, I'm not moving out, Erika," he says.

"Well, I think we need a break from each other and obviously you have some thinking to do," I say.

"Well, I'm not going anywhere. If you think one of us needs to move out, then it's going to be you. I'm not going anywhere," he says. I am absolutely still. There are so many thoughts running through my mind, the first of which is that I don't want my kids to think that I'm the one who left this marriage. If I'm the one to move out, I'm afraid that's exactly what they'll think.

"Why should I be the one to move out when you're the one who fucking cheated on me?" I yell.

"I never cheated on you, Erika," he yells back. "I don't know why you keep saying that."

"Well, I think you're lying to me. And I don't want stay here in this house knowing that. I'll find somewhere to go, and we can tell the kids when you get home," I tell him.

"Whatever," he says, like I'm not going to follow through. "I'm going to get the kids and I'll be back in a little bit."

After he leaves, I try to pull myself together. I don't know how I am going to tell the kids that I am moving out. I have no idea where I am going. I have no idea how long I'll be gone. All I can think of is that I want to make a statement to him that I never want this to happen again. I want him to know that it matters to me. I want him to know that he can't continue a relationship with Shelley and stay in our marriage. I decide to call my aunt Susan. Nobody in my family has any idea about what the hell is going on. She will be the first to know.

"Hey Susan," I say. "It's Erika."

"Well, hi there," she says. "How are you?" "I'm ok," I lie. "I need a favor." "OK," she says, sounding willing.

I take a deep breath.

"I need somewhere to stay for a while," I say. "I don't really know how long. I just know that I don't want to go live at my mom and Dad's house. Would it be ok if I stayed in your basement for a little while?"

Susan and my uncle Kevin, my mom's brother, have two kids, Alicia and John. Alicia is out of the house, living on her own, but John is still in high school and living at home. I don't really want to put them in this position, but I also do not want to go to my parent's house where my mom will be breathing down my neck every day.

"Well, ok," she says. "When are you planning on coming?" "Can I come tonight?" I ask.

"Sure, that's fine," she says. "You can sleep in the back room in the basement."

They have a room that they built in their floor plan that is like a dungeon. There are no windows, and they only use it to watch movies or play video games. It's cold and dark and they're hardly ever down there. I feel like I'll be out of their way down there, and have some space to myself.

"That's perfect," I tell her. "I don't know how long I'll stay but hopefully it won't be too long."

"OK, see you later tonight," she says.

"OK, thanks, Susan," I say. "See you later."

Chapter 13

When Brian gets back from getting the kids, I get emotional just looking at them. Bryce has some way of knowing when something is wrong, like the night he called me when I was at volleyball and Shelley was at our house. I don't know how I am going tell them that I am leaving for a little while. But first I have to tell Brian.

I corner him in the kitchen.

"We need to talk," I say.

"About what?" he asks.

"Well, if you won't be the one to leave, then I will," I say. "I'm moving out tonight. I don't know when I'll be back, but I can't stay here with you knowing that something is going on with Shelley."

Instead of addressing what I just said to him, he just moves on. Instead of reassuring me again that there is nothing going on with her, he turns it around like he's concerned about me.

"Well, where are you going?" he asks.

"I'm going to stay at Susan and Kevin's house, but I don't want the kids to know because otherwise they will want to go with me," I tell him.

"Well, when are you coming back?" he asks.

"I don't know right now, but I can't live this way," I say. "I feel like you're not telling me the truth, and I just need to get away and clear my head."

"OK, well are you going to see the kids when you're gone?" he asks.

"Well, I'll still go to their activities and stuff, but I just won't be living here. I really wish that you would be the one to move out right now," I say.

"Well, I'm not, so move on," he tells me.

"I know, so that's why I have to be the one to do it," I say. "I can't live like this, Brian."

"Like what?" he asks, like the last two days were a dream or something.

"Knowing that you don't even know if you want to be with me or not," I tell him.

"Well, what are you going to tell the kids?" he asks.

"I'm going to tell them that I'm moving out for a while, until we can figure out what's best for our family," I say.

As I turn to leave the bedroom, Bryce startles me standing in the doorway.

"Hey buddy," I say, trying to smooth over my voice.

"What are you doing?" he asks. "Where are you going, mom?" "I'm going to live at Susan and Kevin's house for a little while until your Dad and I can figure out what we're going to do," I say. "Why?" he asks.

"Well, it's complicated," I tell him. "I need to get away so I can think about some things."

It's not really complicated but I don't want to tell him that his Dad cheated on me. I was really not prepared to have this conversation right now. I wish that I could postpone it, forever. But I'm leaving tonight. "Well, when are you coming back?" he asks.

"I don't know yet, buddy," I tell him.

Then Bennett shows up in the doorway with a big smile on his face. I was packing while Brian and I were talking and now I'm holding the bag in my hand.

"Where are you going, mommy?" Bennett says.

I squat down in front of him and grab his hand. It's even harder to tell Bennett because he has no concept of time. He won't understand any of this.

"I'm going to stay with some friends for a while so your Dad and I can have some time apart," I tell him.

I know he wants to ask why, but he says nothing. He's only 7, and I know it won't matter what the answer is anyway. The fact is that his mom is leaving. Now I'm angry because I know I shouldn't be the one to leave. Brian should. I know that the boys will remember this for the rest of their lives. But somehow I hope that someday they will understand why I made this decision. I give each of the kids a kiss and head to the mudroom to get my shoes. Tears are welling in my eyes again. I pray to God I am doing the right thing. I know in my heart that I can't stay and let Brian think that what he's done is OK, but I'm so angry that he's not the one who is leaving. The kids have all followed me. I open the door to the garage and wave goodbye. I can't even speak. There is nothing to say. A real father would not watch his wife leave her children when he should have been the one to go.

Before I even get to the highway, I am sobbing. When I get to Kevin and Susan's house, I politely say hello, thank them for letting me stay, then head to the basement. Susan already has blankets and pillows set out for me. Neither of them asks any questions, but clearly they are uncomfortable with whatever is going on. It is the longest night. I'm supposed to go to work in the morning after having four days off and I just want to crawl into a hole. I feel like the whole damn town knows that my husband cheated on me, and yet nobody says anything and nobody really cares.

Around 9, Susan comes downstairs while I'm watching TV. I'm not even really watching it, just hearing the voices to make some noise because it's so quiet here. Susan sits down in the chair next to the couch I am laying on. She asks me if I want to talk about what is going on. The answer is no, but I feel like I owe her an explanation. I tell her the shortest story that I can to help her understand why I feel like I needed to leave home. She gives me a hug and she tells me she loves me. We've both get tears in our eyes when she turns and goes upstairs. I barely sleep, maybe a couple of hours at best.

The next morning when I get to work, I have an e-mail from Brian.

From: Brian Daniels

To: Erika Daniels

Date: Tuesday, August 24, 2007

Subject: You and Me

Good morning, Erika. I hope that you were able to get some sleep last night. I was up most of the night thinking about everything that has happened. I'm sorry for how I've treated you. I didn't want you to leave, but I didn't want to leave either. I wanted us to both stay and work this out. I know that I haven't always been the best husband and friend to you, but I try every day to love you. And I do love you more and more every day.

These past few weeks have been really crazy, a rollercoaster. I've been confused and you could say that I've been an ass. I'm sure you have. I feel like we are meant to be together, and that somehow we will find a way to work this out. You are the love of my life, my soul mate and best friend. I know that you have only been gone one night, but I miss you already. I want you to come home and be with me and the kids. The kids miss you and I miss you. Please call whenever you want to, and you can come and see the kids anytime.

I love you very much, Erika.

Love, Brian

By the time I reach the end of the e-mail, I am sobbing. My co-worker on the other side of the cubicle hears me and calls over the top of the wall and asks me if I am OK. I tell her that I am, but she knows me better than that. The week drags on. I call the kids every day, but there is nothing like being at home.

Chapter 14

On Sunday afternoon, I miss the kids so badly that I decide to take a drive out to the house. Every light in the house is on and it looks like they are sitting at the kitchen table. I want to pull in the driveway and go inside but I drive past. I turn onto the side road that borders our property and pull into the field drive. I have the radio blaring to drown out my sobbing. I have no idea how long I am sitting there before I see a 4-wheeler come up over the ridge of the pasture out of the corner of my eye. It scares the hell out of me. Brian is driving it. I want to put the car in reverse and drive away, but it's too late. He's pulling up next to the car. His face is somber and I can tell he's been crying. He parks the 4-wheeler, turns off the engine and gets off. My heart skips a beat in that moment, like he's there to rescue me. He walks over to the car and I roll down the window, but he grabs for the handle and opens the door.

"What are you doing way out here," he asks?

"Nothing, just sitting here. I missed you guys so I went for a drive and I ended up here and I was just sitting here thinking about things," I tell him.

"Are you coming home?" he asks.

"No, I can't, Brian," I say.

"Why?" he asks.

"I'm just so sad that you did this," I say through a broken voice. "I don't understand it, and I'm confused, and I'm mad and I'm angry." He's crying now. He tries to grab my hand and I pull away. I don't want him to touch me.

"I know, Erika. I'm sorry, for everything. I don't know what else to say. I love you. You're the love of my life. Will you please just come in the house?" he begs.

"This has been the longest week of my life, being away from you guys. And you should have been the one to leave in the first place." I tell him, angrily.

"I didn't want to leave. And I didn't want you to leave either. I want you to come home," he says.

"I'm so angry. I don't know how you could do this to me, to our family. I honestly don't think I will ever get over this. I don't even want to be near you right now," I say.

"Well, why are you here then?" he asks.

"Because I miss you guys," I say, as tears are streaming down my face.

He drops down to his knees.

"Please stay. I love you. I'm sorry. I don't know what I was thinking. We'll work through it together. I want us to be together, to be a family again," he tells me.

I look away. I want to be home, but I feel like I have to be stronger than staying away from him for six damn days. It feels like it's going to kill me. There is a long silence. Minutes pass.

"Maybe I could just come in for a little while and see the kids," I say.

"Yes," he says. "Whatever. However long you want to stay." For some crazy damn reason, all I can think about is making love with him. A week ago he was telling me that he had feelings for Shelley. Now I want to remind him that I can still fuck like a porn star. I put the car in reverse and head toward the house. Brian meets me in the garage and gives me a long, hard kiss until I pull away. When I get in the house, I'm relieved to be there. Becca runs into my arms and I give her big kisses. The boys are in the basement watching TV. We spend the night together and it feels just like it should, except that I'm not sure I want to be married to my husband anymore.

After we get the kids to bed, I head to our bedroom where Brian is watching TV. It's been weeks since we've had sex and the woman in me wants to tonight. The wife in me never wants to have sex with Brian again. I do my usual going-to-bed bathroom routine and wonder what I'll find when I go out to the bedroom. As I start taking off my clothes and open the drawer to get out my pajamas, Brian says

"Don't. Just come here."

I climb into bed. He is naked, an obvious sign that he wants to have sex. He usually wears boxers to bed. He grabs hold of me with one hand and reaches around to grab my ass with the other. He pulls me into him and gives me a kiss. His penis is hard and ready to go. I'm a little surprised. In an awkward moment, I pull away and tell him that my heart is half in it. He gets on top of me anyway and kisses me passionately then, moving down to my boobs and then my space. I love oral and he's always been very generous with it, but tonight I know I will not be able to focus on that long enough to orgasm anyway. He gives me a gentle kiss, and a little nibble. Before he goes any further, I grab him under his arms and pull him back up on top of me. If I'm ever going to be able to do this, it's going to have to be now. As he eases into me, I grab hold around his back and push him in as far as he will go.

I think about him fucking Shelley. I wonder if it was in the car or against it, on the ground, maybe against a tree. Was it hard and animal-like or long and slow? Was it many times, or only one? Did she suck him off until he came? Did she cum? For a few minutes it consumes me, but somehow, in some crazy way, it makes me more into our sex. I remind myself to focus or I'll never get through it.

I go back to thrusting him into me, my legs open wide and ready to take all of him. We get into a nice rhythm. Then I want to take over control. Without saying a word, I push against his chest and he pulls far enough away from me that I can push the weight of him over and roll on top. He slips out and I help him back in. I find my own rhythm, hard on top and smashing against him. I want to take out all of my frustrations of him fucking Shelley and lying to me about it on his penis. He doesn't seem to mind. I can tell by his face that he's getting close to orgasm. I roll off so he can go hard on top. When he enters me again, he starts to soften. I know in that moment that he fucked Shelley and he either feels guilty about it, or his thoughts have turned to her while he's lying there fucking me. I want to finish this so I push him into me again and he comes back to hard. He thrusts fiercely into me, sucking hard on my nipples until he finishes.

When he pulls out of me, I roll over and away from him, waiting for him to spoon with me for a few minutes like we usually do, but he doesn't. Instead he gets up from the bed and goes to the bathroom.

Chapter 15

*T*he next day at work I find out that there is an Employee Assistance Program that will provide some initial counseling to employees and their families going through hard times. I secretly wonder if this situation qualifies, but decide to call anyway. After I find out some more information, I go home to talk with Brian about it. "So I was thinking that we are probably going to need to do some counseling," I suggest to him as he's watching T.V that night, half listening.

"Well, isn't counseling kind of expensive?" he asks.

I roll my eyes, like that's our worst worry right now.

"Well, there is a program where we can meet with someone three to four times for free and then get a referral somewhere else if we need it," I explain. "Marcus and Janet have gone before." "Well, when can we start?" he asks.

"I don't know," I say. "I just called to get more information but I'm assuming we can get in pretty quickly. I'll call tomorrow and schedule something."

The next day I schedule an appointment for the following day. Brian meets me there. We sit in the waiting room in uncomfortable silence for 15 minutes before our counselor appears from around the corner. She is an older woman, maybe late 50s or early 60s. She walks with a cane and hobbles. She looks a bit eccentric, with reddish hair in a messy spike and horn-rimmed glasses. She is wearing a longer, black full skirt with black boots and a colorful top with ragged edges. She looks like a gypsy of sorts. I immediately worry that Brian will not like her.

"Good morning," she says, reaching out her left hand. I grab it to say hello. Brian grunts his own welcome. I'm already right. He doesn't like her.

When we get back to her office and get settled, she asks us to explain why we're there. I'm thinking this is a great time for Brian to chime in and fess up to everything, but of course, he doesn't.

"Well, a few weeks ago Brian admitted to me that he has feelings for a woman that we've been friends with for a just a few months. Then he stayed out all night with her a couple of weeks ago, but he says that they didn't have sex," I explain.

"And you believe him?" she asks, like he isn't even in the room sitting right next to me.

Oh, how to answer, with my head or my heart, because right now there is a difference. I want to believe him, but I know in my heart he is lying.

"No, I don't," I admit.

"Well, why not?" she asks.

I explain the Sunday morning shower incident. Brian is fidgeting in his chair all the way through the story.

"Well, do you think you'll ever believe him?" she asks me. "I don't know," I admit again. "I just don't understand why, when he had the chance to prove all of my suspicions wrong that he chose not to."

Brian says nothing. He just sits there. She looks at him and back at me.

"Well, let's move on. Why don't you tell me a little bit about your relationship, up until this point," she says, looking at Brian now since I've already done most of the talking. The hint goes straight over his head, or he at least pretends that it does. I look at Brian again, hopelessly waiting for him begin. He says nothing, so I start with the basics.

I tell her that we've been married for 11 years, together for 16. We met when I was 17, and Brian was 18, high school sweethearts, at least for me. We both went away to college and have Bachelor Degrees. I tell her that we were engaged to be married when I got pregnant with our oldest son, Bryce. We decided to keep our wedding date the same so we had Bryce first, then got married, and then built our first house, all in the same year.

Four years later, our second son was born, Bennett. The following year, my Dad's mom died, and then Brian's sister died of cancer. That summer I met my half-sister, Denise. Then Brian's grandma died. The following summer, Becca was born and we bought 40 acres of land to build a house. In the fall we started building and moved in the following spring. After that my panic and anxiety started and I went through my CBT. The next fall we started working on the basement and finished in the spring. The next summer we decided to put the house on the market for a year. When it didn't sell, we took it off. Then we decided we were going to stay in the country and put in the in-ground swimming pool.

I tell her we have dogs. I tell her about our careers. I tell her about our parents and their marriages. Brian chimes in every now and then. When we are done, she looks exhausted. No wonder you're at this place, she says. You haven't slowed down in 11 years of marriage, and as soon as you did, you didn't know what to do with the other, she say. I guess it is the truth, but it doesn't make me feel any better.

We go to a few more sessions with her. Brian doesn't like her and I am busy with a huge project at work. I think I just need time and a

little space. She tells us that what happened between Brian and Shelley was an emotional affair since he has never admitted to having sex with her. She recommends a couple of books that we should read. I read them. She tells us to go on a vacation together. We go up north for our anniversary. She tells us that sometimes it can take up to seven years for a spouse to get over an affair, and sometimes they never do. Brian just rolls his eyes and walks out of her office.

For months and months, it feels like everywhere I go, I collide with Shelley or Cole, or someone in their family. At the grocery store or the bank or the kids' concerts at school. I feel like people look at me differently. I don't really know if anybody knows anything about what is going on with our marriage, but it sure feels like they do.

I throw myself into my job. I have been working on an implementation at work for almost five years and we are nearing completion. I am burnt out. I am depressed. My marriage is in shambles, but I just want to finish the project and then focus on fixing the rest of my life. The project goes live a few months later. It is the greatest career success of my life. After that we are transitioning into maintenance mode at work and things are slowing down. I am ready to move on to something else, and I feel like it would give me a starting point for a fresh start with everything.

Finally in August 2008, a year after Brian and Shelley spent the night together, I accept a huge promotion in a completely different job and department than I had ever been in before. Since Becca is in school, Brian wants me to go back to full-time. It is also more responsibility and a chance to move higher in the organization. It feels like the chance to breakaway and move forward, in more ways than one.

Chapter 16

*I*t is Labor weekend. Marcus is gone on his annual hunting trip to Colorado. He usually misses Janet's birthday. We decide to have a pool party and bonfire that Sunday, and invite some friends over, including Janet and my parents. I am secretly happy that Marcus is gone. All summer long he and I were like fire and gasoline, getting into arguments every time one or both of us had too much to drink. He would start picking on me for some little thing, my hair was crazy or I couldn't drink fast enough or most of the time he'd tell some stupid joke about gays, black people, Hispanics. I just don't tolerate that stuff and I'm not afraid to call him out. Sometimes he'd even pick on Janet, and that put me over the edge every time. It will be nice to have a night without him, to just enjoy Janet and the girls.

We have smores and the kids are running around with leftover sparklers that we have from the 4th of July. Shortly after midnight, I go inside to put the kids to bed. Her girls are already sleeping in the basement. I tuck my kids in. When I come back outside, everybody is gone. Brian and Janet are sitting by the fire. I am tired, ready for bed. I am starting to trust Brian again. I am starting to move past the affair with Shelley. I am making a stronger commitment to myself to try to move on. I feel like this is another chance for me to build trust with him. If I can't trust him with one of my best friends, then I probably can't trust him with anybody.

After one more beer, I head in the house around 12:30. I check on the kids again, go upstairs and do my bathroom routine, and finally hit the pillow around 1 a.m. I wake up at 2 a.m. and look outside. I can see Brian and Janet's shadows sitting by the fire. I go back to sleep. I wake up at 4 and Brian is not in bed with me. I get out of bed and check the campfire, a little panicked but trying to stay calm and not overreact. They are gone from the fire now. I go out to the kitchen, then look in the living room and find Brian lying on the couch. I go downstairs and Janet is sleeping on the air mattress between Becca and Amy. All is well.

In late September, my sister comes to visit to celebrate her birthday. She arrives on a Thursday and is heading out on Monday morning. I make plans to drive to pick her up from the airport so she won't have to rent a car for the weekend. She is my best friend so I am happy to get her all to myself for five whole days, except that I have to share her a little with my Dad.

Denise is my half-sister actually. During my senior year of high school, at dinner one night with my mom and Dad and brother, my parents announced to my brother and I that my Dad had another daughter that was born when he was 19. I was thrilled. I had always wanted a sister. The problem though was that my Dad didn't even know if Denise knew about him. Her mom had married a man named Larry when Denise was only four-years-old. My Dad allowed Larry to adopt Denise to raise her as his own so that she would have as normal life as possible. In the time since my Dad gave up his custody, he would see her occasionally around town because she had family here. But he never spoke to her.

In the summer of 2001, just after Brian's sister died of cancer, Denise called my Dad and wanted to meet him and the rest of our family. She was coming home to visit her sister. It was a little bittersweet for Brian, since he had just lost his sister to cancer and I was just meeting mine for the first time. She and my Dad made plans to meet on a Saturday afternoon. Their first "date" was a canoe trip down the river. It was amazing the connection and chemistry and forgiveness that happened between them during that first visit. I felt like I had known her all my life.

When Denise came that September, I had already known her eight years. I had talked to Denise and Janet about the other so much, but they had never met. And Denise and Janet were my two best friends in the world, so I was really looking forward to spending time with both of them, together.

On Saturday, we make plans to have some friends over to our house to hang out. Marcus and Janet are the first to arrive, and Denise and Janet instantly hit it off. They are both witty and pretty and smart, independent women who know what they want and aren't afraid to go after it. We talk about men and careers and friends. The conversation just flows as we sit by the pool and drink beer and talk.

After a while, the rest of group wants to go for a road trip down toward the river. There is a flood run going on in the river towns with bikers and beer everywhere. Four of us ladies hop in my mom's cherry red Ford Mustang convertible: Mom and me in the front seat, Janet and Denise in the back. The guys hit the road in our Jeep Wrangler 4X4: Brian and Marcus in the front seat, my brother, Dad and Gary in the back. We head toward the river. Our first stop is Bunnie's Bar.

Bunnie's is an older bar, a dive on the inside really. Animal carcasses are plastered all over the walls: deer heads, fish, ducks, a huge moose head, a fox, even an opossum. But the view of the Mississippi River is phenomenal. The establishment sits high on a hill, overlooking a scenic highway that borders the river. There are wide open views of the main channel of the river. Denise's cousin, Barb, actually owns the place, so we figure we might get some free drinks out of the day.

When we walk in, there is a huge crowd hovered around the bar that is set at an angle in the middle of the place. Some of Denise's family is actually there, so she grabs my hand and takes me around to meet some of them on the backside of the bar. The rest of our crew loitered around the bar, waiting to get drinks. Barb is all over us, giving Denise a big hug, and within minutes, we both have drinks. I look around the bar for Janet then, but she's standing outside talking to a man and a woman on a bike outside. A few minutes later she walks in the bar and joins the group. I wave for her to come over by me and Denise, but she just smiles and takes one of the seats at the bar that just opened up. My brother plops down next to her on the left and Brian on the right. It is adorable. My brother is about 5"6' and 250 pounds. Brian is 6'2' and 270. And there, in the middle, is my little friend Janet. She is not even 5 feet tall and 110 pounds soaking wet. I holler across the bar, "Get together, you three. I wanna take your picture."

My brother rolls his eyes.

"C'mon, Erika, do you have to?" he begs.

"Yes," I insist. "Now get together."

The three of them pull together, the men half-heartedly but with their arms wrapped around Janet, who is holding up her bottle of beer with a huge grin on her face. I give them the thumbs up when I take the picture and they relax, taking another drink of their beers in unison. I turn back to Denise who is talking to Barb. A few minutes later, there are shots being poured and served to us by the bartender. I get a Cherry Bomb, my personal favorite. Denise doesn't like them so she re-orders a Jaeg-Bomb. I drink the other Cherry Bomb. I have no idea who even bought them. And the beer and the shots just keep coming for me and Denise. Her family is buying, and Brian and Marcus, my Dad and brother. Before long, a guy on the other side of the bar is definitely flirting with Denise. She looks at him and then back at me. She is a hot, curvaceous 43-year-old, with fake tits and a great ass. Everywhere we go, she gets hit on so it's no surprise.

"He's cute," I tell her, winking. "Go for it. Go buy him a drink." She walks over and starts chatting with him, and I make my way to the other side of the bar where Brian and Janet are talking. My parents, Marcus and my brother are talking to some of the bikers outside.

Brian turns to me as I approach and Janet smiles. The music is blaring.

"Are you ready to go?" he yells.

"Why," I holler back, a little disappointed.

"We need to get a little closer to home. Those guys want to head to Monroe for a little while," he shouts back.

"OK, that's cool," I shout. "Denise is just buying a beer for that guy over there, so let me get her and then we can go."

"OK, we'll meet you outside," he says, as he and Janet head toward the door.

I walk over closer to where Denise is standing and smile as I approach.

"They're ready to go," I say.

She looks at me strangely. Either she doesn't want to leave or she didn't hear me. I lean a little closer into her.

"They want to go to Monroe," I say right in her ear, "Get closer to home."

She stays close and says, "OK, let me finish this beer with him and I'll meet you outside in a few minutes."

She pulls back and looks at me. The guy is watching intently, probably thinking he'd like to be right in the middle of us. I give him a 'dream on' kind of smile, and walk toward the door and head outside. The rest of us are standing outside, talking to some bikers and finishing up our beers when Denise walks out of the bar. She has a huge smile on her face.

"OK," she says. "Let's hit it. He's going to meet us there." I smile back and we head toward the convertible, all of us giggling at her. Denise and I jump in the back. Janet shuts the door so she can hurdle into the front seat. The guys drive out in front of us in the Jeep. They head out on the highway. We're still sitting at the stop sign waiting to cross the 4-lane when Janet stands up in the passenger seat, grabs the bottom of her shirt and bra. She lifts them up over her head, flashing her small but perky bare-breasted B-cups to the Jeep slowly gaining speed 100 yards in front of us. Brian adjusts the rear-view mirror, looking back. Marcus turns around in the passenger seat. Janet is laughing hysterically. My mom looks over at her just as she is putting her shirt back down. She is shocked. I turn to Denise, laughing. "What the hell was that?" she says, looking a little surprised. "How should I know," shrugging my shoulders, smiling. It's definitely out of character for Janet but she hasn't been able to handle her booze for as long as I've known her. Denise laughs. Janet is still cackling as we pull out on the highway behind them, motorcycles flying past us, not knowing the show that they just missed. Alright, lil' mama, that's about enough shots for you, I'm thinking to myself.

When we get to the bar in Monroe about 15 minutes later, the guys are already there standing outside with drinks in their hands. The town sits on a deep valley facing east and doesn't get much sun after 3. The sun is setting and it's cooling down. We are snickering as we climb out of the convertible. Brian and Marcus are both grinning at us as we walk toward them. Marcus walks toward Janet and wraps his arms around her, rubbing her ass.

"What was that about, baby," he says grinning, grabbing her on the backs of her legs and lifting her up. She spreads her legs and locks them around his middle.

"Just a little kiss," she says, giving him a smooch on the cheek.

"Did you like it?" she asks.

"Well, yeah," he answers, "But so did the rest of the folks on the highway."

"Oh, nobody saw me but you," she grins, "Except maybe Brian." He just looks at her, shaking his head, turning it sideways in disapproval.

She turns toward the bar, grasping the door handle and flinging it back hard, wide open until it hits the back of the building. Her head falls back and she roars with laugher, still amused by her performance. We all stand there watching her, wondering how long she is going to last tonight. And 15 minutes later, she and Marcus are already on their way home.

The next day I have to take Denise to the airport. On the way, we're talking about the weekend, funny moments with the kids, the road trip, and time with Dad. Denise gets quiet for a bit so I ask her what is wrong.

"The time just goes by so fast," she says. "I know," I say. "We just have to do this more often." She looks at me curiously.

"What else?" I ask.

She looks at me but doesn't say anything for a moment. "I just don't know what to think about what happened with Janet yesterday," she says.

"I know, it was definitely out of character for her," I confirm. "I've never seen her do something like that before."

"Well, when you think about it, the only one who could actually see her do it was Brian since Marcus was sitting in the passenger seat and the guys in the backseat were facing forward," she says.

"Yeah, that's true," I say, feeling like that's the end of the conversation, but she goes on.

"Well, I wonder why she would even do something like that if he was the only one who could see it?" she says.

I look at her. Now I see what she's getting at.

"I don't know. She was wasted. Just a stupid drunk moment, I guess," I suggest.

"Yeah, I guess," she says.

But I know by the look on her face that she's wondering if there's something more. When we get to the airport, I get out of the car to help her with her bags.

"Love you, sis," she says.

"Love you too," I reply.

"Be cautious, ok?" she says.

"I will," I say. "No worries."

She turns and rolls away with her luggage, and I already miss her as I watch her head up the escalator toward security.

Chapter 17

*T*he following week, Janet e-mails me at work and asks if we want to go along on a trip to Vegas with her and Marcus in October. She has a business trip there, and Marcus doesn't want to fly alone. Flying scares the hell out of him. She will go out a few days early, and then we can come out for the weekend when she is done with her conference. The only problem is that the trip is scheduled for the weekend of our anniversary. I write her back and tell her I will talk with Brian about it and get back to her.

That night when we are lying in bed watching TV, I bring it up. "So Janet asked me today if we wanted to go to Vegas with them at the end of October," I tell him.

"Oh yeah, why is that?" he asks.

"Well, she has a business trip at the end of October, the weekend of our anniversary. Marcus doesn't want to fly alone. You know how he gets. She'll fly out earlier in the week and then we can meet her there," I explain.

"Well, what are we going to do with the kids?" he asks. "Well, between our parents, we can probably get it figured out?" I say.

"Where are they staying?" he asks.

"I don't know. She didn't say. But we've probably got enough miles to get at least one free flight. The only thing that I'm worried about is that the last time we went to Vegas with them, everything we did was about Janet, whatever she wanted to do. I don't want to be following her around like a dog on a leash," I say.

"Well, we'll just have to go off and do our own thing. We don't have to spend every minute with them," he says.

"I know, but we said that the last time too, and then Marcus and I ended up spending most of the time watching you and Janet on the rides," I say. "She's got a way of monopolizing the time. We'll just have to make sure that we have time to ourselves on our anniversary, right?"

"Yeah, we can do something and then meet up with them later. But I don't want to be gone too many days from work, so let's go either Thursday to Sunday or Friday to Monday, whatever is cheaper," he says.

"OK, I'll talk to her tomorrow about it," I tell him.

And I roll over to go to sleep. I don't know how long I was sleeping, but after I bit I feel Brian's hands all over me. He is rubbing my back and my ass. It is usually all it takes to get me in the mood, with guaranteed results. I lay there for a little while as he is rubbing me, not letting him know that I am awake yet. I am thoroughly enjoying it. As wetness forms between my legs, I roll over and ask him what he is doing.

"Nothing," he says with a sleepy smile.

He keeps rubbing me and then slowly moves his hand down the curve of my butt and slips a finger inside of me. Hmm, I moan. I lift my left leg up toward him, touching his rock hard penis. Now I am wide open for him. He rubs my slit and penetrates me again, sliding it in and out. God, I am wet. I lift my ass off the bed then, so he can go deeper. He is fucking me with his big thick fingers and I love it. I am already close to orgasm when he turns me over. He loves to go down on me. He moves his body down on the bed, then grabs my hips and pulls me closer to him. He lowers his face into my wet cunt and starts licking feverishly back and forth over my clit. He slips a finger inside me, and works it gently again until he is all the way in. I can already tell it is going to be a double orgasm kind of night. A few minutes later my back is arching in complete pleasure as he hits my G-spot and my clit is throbbing. Halfway through, I grab his arms to pull him up on top of me. I love to finish together. I grab his ass and push his groin into me as his penis slides inside. He is thrusting and I am quietly moaning in his ear, my orgasm finishing before his.

I have gotten good at being quiet with all of the strange places that we have had sex before. My mind wanders as he is driving his tool into me. Against the sink in a restaurant bathroom, on a bar floor, in a Rent-a-Jon bathroom, paddling down the river in a canoe with my parents a quarter mile ahead of us, on the golf course, in an airplane, against a car in his parent's garage.

Then I come back to the moment. Well, let's just say we'd had our share of public events. He is pulling his body away from me, climaxing. I kiss his neck, and then bend my head to kiss his nipples. He is smiling, and then it is over.

"Wow, that was nice," he says.

I smiled. I was happy.

"I love you," I tell him.

"Love you too."

The next day when I get to work, I e-mail Janet to let her know that we want to go along to Vegas with them. She tells me she is leaving on Monday and her conference is done on Friday morning. She says that they are staying in the suites at the MGM. She says that it is pretty expensive and if we want to stay at the main hotel it will probably be cheaper and just as convenient. We decide to leave late on Thursday and come home Monday. I tell her I will get an airline ticket for Marcus and that they can pay us later.

An hour later, I book 3 tickets to Vegas and 3 nights of freedom to celebrate our 12th wedding anniversary. And the adage, "What happens in Vegas, stays in Vegas" could never have been truer.

The actual flight to Vegas was perfect, with the exception of Marcus who is a nervous wreck, sweating profusely, talking loudly and drunk on screwdrivers. Janet picks us up in her rental car, and the look on her face suggests that she is less than impressed. Marcus reeks of booze as we hop in the car.

"Good grief," Janet says. "How many drinks did you have, baby?" "I don't know," he slurs. "Me and Brian had a few," smiling. I chime in with, "Well, those two sat together and Marcus met

some guys who were Green Bay fans, and he was talking their ears off."

Brian just smiles watching Marcus.

"Well, let's get going," Janet says. "I've been waiting to start drinking until you guys got here."

And that's just what we did, for 3 days straight.

Brian and I decide to go to a Brazilian steakhouse the night of our anniversary. I feel badly leaving Janet and Marcus out of our plans so we invite them along. The dinner is amazing and we are half drunk when we get done. We toast to our anniversary and to a fun trip, since we are leaving tomorrow. At the end of dinner, when the waitress brings the check, Marcus grabs it quickly to pay for it.

"No, that's not necessary, you guys," Brian says to him.

"Yes, we insist," Janet says. "It's not negotiable. You invited us along for dinner on your anniversary and we're getting the tab."

"Really, you don't need to do that," I tell them.

"I told you, not negotiable," she says again. "So what do you want to do now?" Janet asks, in a drunken giggle.

Brian and I look at each other, shrugging our shoulders, both thinking we'd like to just go back to our room and screw. Here we go again, I think. Janet might as well throw a leash around our 3 necks and drag us down Las Vegas Boulevard on parade.

"We could go to Mandalay Bay and see Sophie," she offers. "I talked to her the other day and she was going to put our names on the VIP list at the lobby of the bar."

Hmm, this could get interesting. Sophie is the same age as me, the sister of Janet's good friend Samantha, and the ex-girlfriend of my brother. She was dating my brother when he lived with Brian when we were first dating. We were all going to different colleges at the time.

I was in my first year at a private Catholic college near St. Cloud, an hour north of the Twin Cities; Brian, at the University of Minnesota; my brother, at the Minneapolis College of Art and Design; and Sophie, at the University of St. Thomas. We spent a lot of time together that year, drinking and eating and cooking and playing cards, just hanging out. Things with my brother and Sophie ended during our junior year of college and she moved to Las Vegas shortly after college graduation. I had not seen her since. She'd had a lot of different jobs while she was was in

Vegas, but at the time, she was working as a bartender in the bar at the top of Mandalay Bay.

"Sure, sounds good to me," I say. "But let's get a cab because Mandalay Bay is on the other end of the strip and it will take us two hours to get there if we walk."

As we head toward the door, the guys want to get a drink in their hand so we stop at the bar, and then we head outside to hail a cab.

When we get to Mandalay Bay, Janet leads us into the hotel and we find the lobby of the bar. It is located at the base of a set of elevators in the middle of the hotel. The bouncer finds Janet's name on the VIP list and the doors of the elevator next to us automatically open, startling me. We step into the elevator, and the doors close fast right in front of me. We rise quickly up 17 stories to the top of the hotel. When the doors open and we step out, it is like walking into a different world.

To the right of us there is a doorway that opens to an enormous room with tables and chairs. There are a few people sitting in there and a sign pointing to the patio straight ahead. To the left, there is a wall that curves around, cornering around to a room with a fireplace in the center of the wall and 3 brown leather sofas centered around a dark wood square coffee table. Around the corner is a huge bar, 30 feet long. And there, in the middle of the bar, stands the blonde-haired, blue-eyed, beautiful Sophie. She is busy behind the bar, which is full of customers all the way across. She doesn't notice us right away. We stand there for a few minutes until the bar clears. She is bent over cleaning some bar glasses, and then she picks up her head and sees us.

An enormous smile comes across her face and she stands up.

"Oh my gosh," she shouts. "How are you guys?" her eyes shining, her face beaming. She looks at each one of us quickly and then her eyes come back to Janet. "I'm so glad you got in touch with me. How is your trip going?"

"It's great," Janet tells her. "We just ate at the Brazilian steakhouse at Stratosphere, and it was fantastic."

"Well, that's great. I've heard good things about that place," she says, then pauses. "So, what can I get you to drink?"

We each order a beer, except Marcus who is fond of Vodka-Mountain Dews, especially when he doesn't really need any more to drink.

"You should go out on the patio. It overlooks the whole strip and it's the best view of the city. It's beautiful out there," she tells us.

Brian stays back and pays the bill, and the three of us head out to the patio. When we get there, she is right. It is breathtaking. You can see all of the hotels on the opposite side of the strip up to the Flamingo, and most of the south side of the city. We stand there a few minutes, saying nothing. Then Brian walks up behind us.

"Isn't it beautiful?" Janet turns and says.

"Yeah," he says, peering over the edge and putting his hand on my back.

There is a couple standing next to the glass railing taking a picture.

"Would you mind taking a picture of the four of us?" I ask.

"Sure," the woman replies as I hand her my camera.

We pose, ladies in the center, and the lights of the city in the background. She hands the camera back to me.

"Ready for another drinky drink?" Marcus asks.

"Nope, I'm good," I say.

"Yep, but I want something from the bar this time," Janet says.

"So I'll go get'em."

"I'll have a Brandy Coke," Brian tells her. He reaches in his pocket to get some money.

"We got it, our treat for your anniversary," Janet says, as she walks away to get our drinks.

I'm not going to argue with either of them when they're drunk. The three of us stand there, overlooking the city. Marcus starts chatting with some folks that are part of a big group that just came out on the patio. Brian and I are sitting at a table, just relaxing and enjoying our drinks. Janet comes around the corner with her hands full, a big smile on her face.

"How much was it," I ask?

"Nothing," she says.

"What?" I say. "What do you mean, nothing? Why?"

"Sophie said that as long as we drink bar rails all night, she can give them to us free. I brought you a Margarita, on the rocks" Janet says, winking. "But we need to tip her, so I gave her $5."

"Wow, perfect," I say as I raise the glass, with a beer in my other hand. "I'll drink to that," and the three of us cheers.

We hang out on the patio, and the drinks are flowing. Brian goes and gets the next round, followed by me. Marcus is drinking two to our one. Janet goes to get another round, and when she comes back, Marcus is passed out in a chair on the other end of the patio, teetering like he's going to fall off of it. She walks over to him and pushes him on the arm.

"Marcus, wake up," she says.

She turns and looks at us. She is pissed off.

"Wake up," she says again, poking him.

He falls sideways. The wrinkles on Janet's forehead are strained and her lip is quivering. She grabs him by the shoulders and pushes him back to center, hoping that he won't fall over. She shakes her head with her hands on her hips as she walks back toward us.

"Well, what are we going to do with him now?" she asks.

I say nothing. There is music blaring over our heads and I don't feel like screaming anymore. It's 1:30 in the morning and I'm ready to go home.

"We'll get him up," Brian says, optimistically. "He just needs a little time. Let him sleep a while."

It irritates me that Marcus has once again gotten smashed and cannot even function. And once again, Brian is going to bail him out of whatever troubles he gets into.

"I'm ready to go home," I tell him.

Janet looks at me, then back at Marcus.

"You guys go ahead," she says. "I'll be fine."

"No, I'm not leaving you here alone with him," Brian says. "You'll never get him home."

She walks back over to Marcus.

"C'mon, Brian," I say, grabbing for his arm. "We're both wasted and it's time to go home."

"I'm not leaving Janet here alone when Marcus is drunk," he says.

"Why? She'll be fine. She would leave me here alone with you if you were sitting in that chair right now," I tell him confidently.

"No, she wouldn't," he says, defiantly.

"Yes, she fucking would. She would leave me here alone and I would get you home and it would be fine," I say.

I'm crying now. The booze is definitely getting to me. I wish I had stuck with beer.

"C'mon, please," I say, begging, screaming over the music. "Let's go."

"No, I'm not leaving," he says.

I am so angry at him. I feel like every time I need him to support me as his wife he can't do it. I understand that we came with Marcus and Janet, but I still don't feel like we are responsible for getting them home. I am his wife and I am ready to go home. It reminds me of the night that he wouldn't go home with me from the bar at home, the night that he left with Shelley. It enrages me and I turn and walk toward the bar.

I hear Brian yell, "Where are you going?"

I say nothing and just keep walking. I don't know where I am going but I need a timeout. I need to figure out what I want to do with this situation. And I hate that I am crying like a God damn baby. I walk to the elevator and when the doors close I stand there for a moment, not sure what to do. Then I push the button to the lobby and the elevator car starts dropping, fast again. My feet start tingling and I don't know if it's the booze or anxiety, probably both. When I reach the bottom, the doors open and the bouncer is standing at the podium. He picks up his head from his VIP list and looks over at me. I'm sure I look like I mess and I try not to scowl at him. After all, he hasn't done anything to bring this on. There is a bench on the other side of the lobby and I head over and sit down.

"Everything ok?" he asks, as if he doesn't know the answer.

"Yep," I lie, my voice shaking.

We sit there in silence for what seems like forever. I'm sure it isn't more than 5 minutes. I can't stand it. I just want to go home, to our hotel room. I just want Brian to go with me. And I can't see far enough in front of what I'm doing to see that I am being really selfish. I stand up and head back over to the elevator. I stand there a moment before the doors open. As I step inside, I turn to the bouncer again and smile to thank him. The doors close and I head back to the bar.

When I step out of the elevator, I don't even know where I want to go. I walk around the curved wall and go sit on one of the couches by the fireplace. I don't even look around before I sit down, but I look around at the people sitting on the couches, and I'm certain that they are probably prostitutes. There is a couple opposite me on another couch. The woman is dressed like a school girl, with a plaid dress, white stockings, red shoes, and her hair in pigtails. The man is balding with a beer belly, wearing a white polo shirt and baggy khakis. She is sitting across his lap, and his hand is creeping up her leg, rubbing slowly. She is giving him the biggest damn fake smile that she's got, and he looks like a high school principal who needs to retire. After a few minutes of me watching them, they get up from the couch and walk through an entryway on the left side of the fireplace.

On the other couch, there is a couple sitting close, right next to each other. She is wearing Goth makeup, dark lips and eyes, straight black hair, a long black dress and black boots. Her eyes are piercing green, close to mine. The man is dressed in a ridiculous-looking Hawaiian shirt and denim shorts. Even more ridiculous are his shoes; a pair of navy blue boat shoes with white laces. They are both thin. In fact, I can see the veins in her arms and I'd probably win a bet that she'd done some heroin pretty recently. I guess you do whatever it takes to get through it when you have to fuck men like that for a living. Shortly, they get up and disappear behind the same entryway as the first couple. Oh dear God, I do not need to know what is going on here.

Then, after sitting alone for a few minutes, I get up and start walking back to the patio to find Brian. As I turn to walk into the adjoining room before the patio, I find Brian and Janet holding each other in an embrace that seems to be more than just a hug between friends. Janet's face is buried in his chest and her arms are not up around his shoulders like a typical hug between friends. Their arms are joined at the sides and her hands are holding him underneath his arms. For a moment I think that they may have been kissing. My eyes squint like they do when I'm angry. I stand there a moment, taking it all in, not believing my eyes.

Brian pulls away from her and turns and looks at me, a look of surprise on his face. Janet's mouth is half-open, apparently speechless.

"What in the hell is going on here," I scream.

"Nothing," Brian says, nonchalantly. "Nothing, Erika," as he steps closer to me.

"Well, it sure as hell doesn't look like nothing," I yell.

I look back and forth between them.

"What the fuck?" I say, waiting for an explanation. I get nothing more.

In a complete rage, I grab my purse, lower my body a little to build up momentum, and hurl it up in the air and sideways across Brian's head. He tries to move to miss it, but I was right on. I hit him just above his temple. Damn, I'm a good shot. Janet steps back to try to avoid getting hit herself. In the moment, I seriously consider moving toward her and clocking her too.

Then Brian shouts, "What in the hell are you thinking?"

"What am I thinking? Don't you mean what you are you thinking?"

I scream back.

Janet hollers, "What the hell, Erika?"

"Don't even look at me," I say, looking at Janet. "You make me sick."

I turn back and look at Brian, holding my gaze for what feels like forever.

"Let's go," I scowl. "We're leaving. Right now."

He turns and looks at Janet like she should try to stop him from going with such a psycho. I start walking. I'm going with or without him, guessing it will be without. When I get to the elevator, I am surprised when he is suddenly standing beside me. When we get in the elevator, on the way down I am singing 'Love in an Elevator' in my head. It's just like me to be horny at a time like this. I guess that's our kind of love.

Chapter 18

*T*he next day our flight doesn't leave Las Vegas until that evening.

Yesterday, we made plans with Marcus and Janet to spend the day by the pool. After what happened last night, that is the last thing I want to do. In fact, I'd like to re-schedule our flight so I don't even have to see Janet today. I have no idea how or if they even got home and I don't really care. When Brian and I got back to our hotel room at 3 a.m., we went straight to bed.

At 8:30 that morning, we wake up to Brian's cell phone ringing.

It's Marcus. I'm lying close enough to Brian that I can hear everything he says. He asks what happened to us. He asks what time we got home. He boasts that he already has a drink in his hand. He asks Brian what time we want to meet at the pool. Brian just looks at me, saying nothing at first. I shake my head at him, hoping that he knows what that means. Of course, Marcus has no idea about what happened the night before. I know that Brian and Janet are not going to tell him, and I'm not ready to. I'm not sure if I ever want to tell him. But I do know that I do not want to go sit by the pool all day with Janet and fake how pissed off I am about what happened last night. I am going to need some time to think about it. Brian tells Marcus that we are going to grab some breakfast and that we will meet them at the pool over by their room after that. As he hangs up the phone, I am getting ready to go to breakfast, without my swimsuit on. Brian is watching me.

"Don't you want to get breakfast and then go straight to the pool from there?" he asks.

"I don't want to go to the pool at all," I say, glaring at him.

"Are you still mad about last night, or what?" he asks, his voice raising.

"What do you think, dumbass?" I scream back at him. "I go down to the lobby to give myself a timeout because you won't go home with me, your own fucking wife, and when I come back, I find you and my best friend in an awkward embrace, and when I ask you what the hell is going on, neither of you has a thing to say."

"What did you want me to say," he asks.

"Well, the truth would be good," I reply. "What the fuck. You can't tell me that a hug like that wasn't something more. It almost looked like you were kissing."

He gets a surprised look on his face. For a moment, I wonder if they had been kissing and he thought that I saw them.

"Well, we weren't," he says. "She's my best friend's wife, for God's sakes. Do you really think I would do that to Marcus?"

"I would hope not," I respond.

He gets up from the bed and walks over to the mirror.

"Jesus Christ, Erika! Look at my fucking head. You clocked with me your fucking purse and I was just telling her goodbye and wishing her luck with getting Marcus home," he shouts at me. "I can't believe that you expected her to get Marcus home by herself."

I don't even look at his head.

"Well, I'm telling you, if it was the other way around, she would have done the same damn thing," I say confidently. "I don't even know what to think about this. God, Brian, I was just starting to get over everything with Shelley, just starting to trust you again."

"Fuck, Erika," he yells. "Are you ever going to forgive me for that?

It was over a year ago and you just keep coming back to it."

I turn and walk toward the bathroom, tears in my eyes. As I walk past him, I see the huge shiner on the side of his head, close to his right eye.

"Oh my God," I say, reaching out to touch it.

He moves away from me.

"Don't touch me," he says, sounding disgusted.

"I'm sorry I did that," I tell him, half-heartedly. I'm more glad that I didn't really hurt him.

"No, you're not," he shoots back.

"Yes," I say. "I really am."

"So what do you want to do today then?" he asks. "Do you want to go sit at the pool with them, or what?"

"I don't know right now," I answer. I look at him and close the door to the bathroom.

I get in the shower. I'm thinking about all of the little moments that Brian and Janet have spent alone together during our marriage. Times they have invited us over for drinks and Brian would go without me.

Times when Brian would go over and hang out with Marcus and then Janet was probably home. Brian even hunted with Marcus, sometimes behind their house on their property, and they would hang out at their house afterwards. The night by the bonfire in September when I went to bed early, Janet's birthday. That night was my first conscious effort to try to let go of Brian and Shelley's fling, whatever is was. It was my first effort at really giving him a chance to re-build trust. And now it just seems all wrong.

I feel like I might be overreacting to what happened, but they were clearly in an embrace that was more than I was comfortable with. And their silence when I asked them what was going on was not reassuring my fears. I have so little trust in Brian at this point that I feel like I need to base my feelings on my relationship with Janet. For goodness sakes, we are Jenna's godparents. I have known her for all of our marriage.

Brian has known her in high school when she and Marcus starting dating when she was 15. Marcus is one of Brian's best friends. Janet is one of mine.

Ten minutes later, I finish my shower, brush my teeth and decide to leave my hair wet and shelf the makeup for the day. When I walk into the hotel suite, Brian is texting on his phone.

"They want to know if we're going to meet them," he says.

I turn toward him, wanting to stall before I answer.

"Well, what do you want to do?" I ask.

"It's up to you," he responds.

But I know it isn't. I'm going to have to deal with this sooner or later. I want to know how they behave when we get there and they are both sober. I want to see how they behave today, after all of this has happened. I decide that if it was really nothing, then sitting by the pool for the day shouldn't be a problem for either of them.

"That's fine," I say. "We'll meet them there, but I want to get some breakfast first. I'm starving."

He grabs his phone and texts back. He's still texting 5 minutes later after I'm dressed and ready to go.

"Now what? Who are you texting now?" I ask.

He looks at me, sternly. Apparently, it's none of my business, again.

"It's Bryce just saying hi, for God sakes," he says.

"OK, well are you ready to go?" I ask.

He's really irritated now. He glares at me, then heads to the door, opens it and steps out into the hallway without me as the door slams in my face.

When we get to the pool, Marcus and Janet are already there.

They are on the opposite side of the pool area. Janet waves as we start walking over. Marcus is chatting with some people who are sitting nearby. We grab some towels along the way. As we get closer, Janet sits up in her chair, grabbing her margarita and taking a sip, then fixing the tie on her black string bikini.

"What have you two lovebirds been doing this morning?" she asks, giggling. Apparently she's had a lapse of memory too or it really is nothing.

I don't say anything, looking at Brian for a response. I'd love to untie her swimsuit but I figure my husband would likely enjoy it. I busy myself rearranging my lounge chair and laying out my towel. He tells her we had breakfast. She responds by going on and on about her night with Marcus. First about their travels back to the hotel, then what time they got home, followed by what time they went to bed, what time they got up, and on and on. I settle on my chair and tune her out. Marcus turns around from his conversation with the pool neighbors and starts talking. Perfect, I won't have to say a word all day. Now all I need is a margarita to go with the salt from last night.

Chapter 19

When we get home from Vegas, I have to leave on a business trip for a conference in Orlando a few days later. It feels like good timing. I need to have some time away from Brian to think about what happened in Vegas. I need to decide what to do with my friendship with Janet. It won't be easy to end our friendship if Brian and Marcus intend to stay friends. And I know that if I don't tell Marcus what happened in Vegas, then nothing is going to change between them. On the morning I am leaving, Brian corners me in the bathroom.

"Erika, while you're gone on your trip, I'd like you to think about if you even want to be married to me anymore," he says. "I can't keep living like this way. You can't keep going back to what happened over a year ago. We have to start moving forward."

I look at him in disbelief. His face is so serious. His voice is shaking.

Tears are swelling in his eyes. Mine too. I don't know what to say.

"Well, what do you want me to do?" I ask.

"I just want you to think about if you want to be married anymore, because right now, it just doesn't feel like you do."

Well, well, well. He's been with Shelley, and now there's maybe something going on with Janet, and he has the balls to ask if I'm the one who doesn't want to be married anymore. What the hell.

On the flight to Orlando, my thoughts are so scattered. Before we're even in the air, I am crying, tears streaming down my face. I turn on my player and crank it up, skipping through the songs feverishly; trying to find one that will help me find the answer to the question I am supposed to answer when I get back in four days.

While I'm there, I try to focus on the sessions, try to compartmentalize my marriage from my work. But I've got four days to figure out what I want to do. I've been given a deadline for my marriage. Perfect. The writer in me loves a good deadline, but this time, there is a lot more on the line than getting an 'A' on a paper. I drink every night, heading to the hotel lobby bar two nights, and the other ordering a bottle of wine in my room with room service. I want to write, but I don't know where to begin. I need more time. The pressure is starting to get to me. The anxiety of the decision is weighing on me.

I call home and talk to the kids on Thursday night. Bryce answers the phone. When I'm done talking with the kids, I ask Bennett if Brian wants to talk to me. He says no. My heart sinks. I'm supposed to leave in the morning, but I'm up all night. In the morning, my eyes are red, aching and tired, barely functioning from my lack of sleep. I skip the morning session of the conference, hurrying on to the airport in an anxious frenzy to get home. I don't know why. I have no idea what I'm going to say to Brian when I get there.

When I get home that night, it's late. The kids are already asleep. I give them a kiss good night and head to our bedroom. The television is on, but thankfully Brian is asleep. I turn off the television and crawl into bed, hoping to avoid any conversation.

"How was your trip," he whispers, sleepy. He startles me.

"It was good," I lie.

"How was your week with the kids," I ask.

"Good. Busy," he says. Then nothing.

"Good night," I say.

"Night."

In the morning, I think I'm in the clear on deciding whether or not I want to be married anymore. I'm on the computer in the kitchen checking the weather for the weekend when Brian comes around the corner. He's standing over me, watching me.

"So did you think about what we talked about the other day while you were away," he asks, putting his hand on my shoulder.

I shiver. Suddenly I don't know what I want.

"I don't know, Brian. I don't know if I can ever get over this. I feel like there is something more that happened with you and Shelley that you aren't telling me. You had the chance to prove me wrong and you chose not to. I want to be married," I reassure him. "I just don't know if I'll ever get over you being with Shelley. And being in Vegas just brought all of the old feelings back."

"Nothing happened between me and Janet in Vegas, Erika," he says. "It was nothing."

"It's not about that anymore. It's about trust," I remind him. "I love you, and I want to be married to you, but if I can't trust you, I don't know how we can ever make it work."

"I'm trying to earn back your trust, but it's been well over a year and we're right back to where we started," he says. "You aren't letting it go."

"Let's just get through Christmas and then decide," I suggest. It's the middle of November and my birthday is two days away, deer hunting a week and Thanksgiving only two. I pause, before I say something that has been on my mind since we got back from Vegas.

"You know, if things don't work out with us, have you ever thought about getting together with Janet? I mean, she's everything you've always wanted. Funny, witty, smart. She just goes with the flow, rolls with things. She's happy all the damn time."

He looks rejected. That is not what I intended. There is some truth to the perfection of the two of them being together, as twisted as it seems. I know he loves her friendly, happy-go-lucky nature, her ability to make people feel at ease, make them laugh. She is the typical homecoming queen, always a smile, with diplomacy and grace, and a bit of a façade, even with the people closest to her, even me.

"What are you thinking, saying something like that?" he scowls.

"That's just stupid."

"You're right," I confirm. "I'm sorry. Let's just get through the holidays, through the cruise with the kids, and then we can talk about this again, ok?"

And I'm praying that the mango Margaritas that I'm going to drink on that ship can drown my sorrows, and fix a marriage that feels like it's over.

Chapter 20

*I*t is the end of December, almost 2009. We just got back from our cruise with the kids. We haven't even been home two hours when Marcus calls to invite us over for a New Year's Party. After what happened in Vegas, I am keeping my distance from them. I can tell it is Marcus on the phone by the way that Brian is talking to him.

"Sure," he says. "What do you want us to bring?" and then, "OK, sounds good," as he hangs up.

"What was that all about?" I ask.

"Marcus and Janet are having a bunch of couples over for a New Year's Eve Party," he says.

He mentions a few that are invited.

"So what do we have to bring," I ask.

"Just some wine, and maybe a bottle of champagne if we want to," he says.

Brian arranges for his parents to have the kids that night. Around 4, I take a bath and he runs the kids over to their house. When he gets back, I'm almost ready to go. He comes in the bathroom, and grabs me from behind, pushing his groin into me. I'm already dressed, and really not in the mood, so I pretend to ignore him.

"We better get going," I say.

He reaches his hands around to cup my breasts.

"We don't have to be there for an hour," he says.

"Well, I'd like to get there before everyone else does," I tell him.

He drops his hands in defeat.

"OK, well, let's get going, then," he says.

I grab a couple of bottles of wine from the rack in the kitchen, a Gewurtzameiner that I bought for when Janet comes over, and a Zinfandel for the rest of the crowd. When we get there, Janet isn't her usual bubbly self. This is the mood that I've seen since we got back from Vegas. A little quiet, subdued. I lean into her and give her a hug, since she looks like she needs one. We pour a glass of wine and head to the couch in the living room. We talk about the kids, jobs, and the usual stuff. Her and Marcus seem different these days, like their relationship is maturing, changing. For as long as I can remember, she has been waiting for him to slow down, to grow up, to be a family man. It seems like he's making his way there, slow but sure. Brian and Marcus are standing at the kitchen counter chatting. I'm alone with Janet for about 15 minutes before other couples start showing up. We're close enough friends with Marcus and Janet that things are different when we are alone with them. Janet puts on her happy face. Soon the house is full of people. A couple of Marcus' sisters are there, Dave, Gary and Julie, Janet's friend Stacy from work, and our friends Steve and Sara get there just as we're sitting down for dinner.

Marcus makes steak on the grill and Janet makes her famous creamed peas and potatoes. It's a fantastic dinner. Afterward we're all just sitting around chatting. The wine and conversation are flowing.

Around 11 o'clock, I look over at Brian talking to Janet's friend Stacy.

They are standing close together, alone, across the room, and away from the rest of the crowd. It's strange to me, as I can't really remember that Brian has ever met Stacy before tonight. She leans into him, whispering something in his ear. Alright, now I'm irritated. I don't feel like my husband should be hearing secrets from a woman that he just met tonight. I keep watching them, and then Stacy turns and sees me. She slowly backs away, as if I won't notice the change in behavior.

Then she says something to Brian that makes him back away too. She finishes her wine and starts walking toward the kitchen. I'm watching her until she looks at me, and then I look away, wondering what in the hell that is all about.

Before I know it, it's 11:45 and Janet gets out the hats and noisemakers and confetti. Crazy girl. Why in the world would she want that confetti shit all over her house? At midnight, Auld Lang Syne is playing on the radio. Janet insists that each couple take a turn under the mistletoe that hangs between the kitchen and the hallway to the mudroom. How romantic, I'm thinking to myself. A kiss from my husband with a bunch of people watching us, but I'm a good sport, and I do it anyway. It's funny as I'm watching the other couples. Some men bend their wives backwards in an awkward pose; others slip their wives the tongue. One husband picks his wife up off the ground, holding her while they kiss. Ours is a quick peck, and I'm hoping that it's fast enough that Janet can't even get a picture of it, but no such luck. She snaps it quickly "Aww, that's cute," she says, pulling the camera in to look at the picture. She's trying to sound sincere but comes across as sarcastic.

Right after midnight, a few couples leave to get home to their kids. I'm drunk and ready to go home, but Brian wants to stay. I slow down my drinking, knowing that I'll have to drive home. An hour later, there are just 8 of us that have stayed. It's 1:15 in the morning, and I'm subtlety begging Brian to leave. In a moment, he goes over to the kitchen, picks up our friend Steve's wife and sets her up on the sink.

Then, she wraps her legs around him and he is simulating having sex with her, pumping his groin into her as we all watch. My mouth drops open. What in the hell is he doing? And now I am definitely ready to go home. Embarrassed and completely pissed off, I tell Brian it's time to go. I guess it must be obvious to him that I'm serious because he says nothing and heads over to the mudroom and starts putting his shoes on. I politely tell the group good night and we head out the door.

On the way home, I am driving and have had enough to drink that I need to concentrate on the road rather than yell at my husband for what just happened at the party. I can hardly hold my sharp tongue.

When we get in the house, though, I come unglued.

"What in the fuck was that all about, Brian?" I say as I follow him back to our bedroom.

"What," he says, like he has no idea what I'm talking about, and there is absolutely nothing wrong with what he just did.

"You just simulated having sex with Sara on the kitchen sink while the rest of us watched," I say.

"Yeah, big deal," he says.

"You've got to be kidding me. What if I would have done that with Steve?" I ask.

"You flirt with Steve all the time," he says.

"Really? Like flirting with Steve and what you just did with Sara are the same thing? I don't think so," I tell him.

"You might as well have just fucked her, Brian, right there in front of God and everyone," I scream at him.

"Yeah, whatever," he says as he turns to walk into our bathroom.

"It's nothing, just like Shelley," I say.

He stops and turns around. His eyes are crazy and his cheeks are red. I don't know if it's from the liquor or the anger, but I am suddenly scared. He grabs me with both hands by the side of the face, hard.

"Ouch! What the fuck was that for? Get your hands off me," I say, as I grab his hands.

In the heat of the moment, the top prong of my wedding ring comes across his face and cuts the space between his lip and his nose.

He's bleeding.

"God dammit, Erika, that fucking hurt," he screams at me. He wipes his hand across his face. When he pulls his hand away, there is blood smeared across it. "I'm tired of you bringing up the Shelley thing."

"Really, Brian," I say. "I'm tired of everything, all of this."

"It's been almost two fucking years. Are you ever going to move on?" he asks me.

"I don't know," I say, "But what you did tonight sure isn't helping."

He grabs each side of my arms, hard again. I know I'm going to have bruises. It won't be the first time, but I've never been afraid of him like this. He pushes me back and then, screaming, he lunges at the space between the closets, punching his fist through the wall. He winces and then turns back at me. He looks at me likes it's my fault. For a moment, I think he's going to punch me. He comes toward me, and I back up.

Then he hollers something, and turns to go into the bathroom. There is a 4 to 5 inch hole in the plaster between our closet doors.

"Oh my God, Brian, what are you doing?" I ask. "You just punched a fucking hole in the wall."

"You just can't let it go, Erika. Every time we're drinking, you get home and just rub the whole Shelley thing in my face," he says.

"Brian, this started with you tonight, taking Sara and throwing her up on the sink and acting like you were going to fuck her right then and there. You should have seen her face. She was mortified."

He walks in the bathroom. I am terrified and walk out of the bedroom, into the kitchen. I pick up the phone to call Brian's Dad to come over. I know that one of us needs to leave and neither of us can drive.

Marilyn answers with her usual, "Nnn, hello," in a sleepy voice.

"Hi Marilyn, it's Erika. Is Tim there?" I ask.

"Yes, just a minute," she says. "Is everything alright?"

"No, Brian and I got into a fight and I need him to come over and get him," I tell her.

I can hear her in the background relaying what I just said. Tim gets on the phone.

"Hello," he says. "Erika?"

"Hi, Tim," I say. My voice is trembling. "Tim, I need you to come over and help me settle Brian down. We got into a fight when we got home from Marcus and Janet's house, and we're drunk, and he punched a hole in the wall in our bedroom."

"Well, where is he now?" Tim asks.

"He's in the bathroom, I think. I don't know. I'm in the kitchen. Can you please just come over?" I ask.

"Yeah," he says. "I'll be over as soon as I can."

In all the years that I have known Brian, his Dad is the only one who can get him to settle down when he is belligerently drunk like this. I know I am doing the right thing. As I hang up the phone, I hear our bedroom door open and Brian starts walking toward the kitchen.

"Who were you talking to," he demands.

"I called your Dad to come over," I tell him, sheepishly.

"Why?" he screams at me. "You're lying. You called the cops, didn't you?"

I have no idea why he said that. For all the drunken arguments and fights that we have had, I have never once called the cops. Somehow, we have always been able to handle it on our own. But for some reason, tonight that stupid man thinks we need to get the law involved. In fear, I back away from him and walk over by the dining room table.

"No, I called your Dad and he is on his way over here right now," I say again.

"You fucking liar," he says.

He is on one side of the table now and I am on the other.

"Why would I lie to you? I called him because neither of us can drive and I don't want to be alone with you right now. You're scaring me. I've never seen you like this before," I say.

"I'm scaring you?" he asks, reaching out his hands to me. "I'm sorry, come over here."

"No," I say, moving to the opposite side of the table.

"Why not," he says, moving closer to me, grabbing onto one of the kitchen chairs. He is irritated. "I just want to give you a hug. What's wrong with a husband wanting to give his wife a hug?" as tears are rolling down his face.

"Nothing is wrong with it, but I'm scared of you right now." I move farther away from him so I am directly opposite of him again. "You just punched a hole in the wall of our bedroom."

"Well, you just cut me with your God damn ring," he says.

He picks up the kitchen chair and slams it on the ground, busting it into pieces.

"I didn't mean to. I was trying to get your hands off of me. You were hurting me," I say.

"Well, great, Erika. Let's call the cops then. You're scared of me,"

he says, like I'm being a baby.

I'm crying now, realizing that he just broke the kitchen chair. He walks over to pick up the phone. He enters numbers into the phone and holds it to his ear.

"Yes, hello? My wife wants to report a domestic assault," he says.

"Oh my God, Brian. What are you doing? I never told you I wanted to call the cops," I tell him.

He looks at me, eyes piercing. At first I think he is faking it, but then I can actually hear a voice on the other end of the line.

"My wife and I just got home from a party and we got into an argument and I grabbed her and punched a hole in the wall and busted a kitchen chair," he tells the dispatcher.

He is listening to the person on the other end. I am crying, trying to be quiet.

"Yes, she is afraid of me." He tells her our address. "OK, here she is."

He holds the phone out for me to take it. I refuse, which infuriates him even more.

"I don't want to talk to them," I say.

"Just do it, Erika. Do it for the kids," he says, handing me the phone.

Grabbing it, I say "Hello?"

"Yes, ma'am. This is the Sheriff's Office," she says. "We're sending an officer out to your address," repeating the address back to me.

"That's not necessary," I tell her. "Everything is fine. I called Brian's Dad to come out here and he'll be here any minute."

"I'm sorry, ma'am, but we have to send an officer to investigate when we get a call like this," she tells me. Now I'm really angry. What an idiot.

"OK, thank you," I say, hanging up the phone. I cannot believe he just did that. He just called the cops on himself. "What in the hell are you thinking?"

Out of the corner of my eye, I see headlights. Brian looks toward the driveway. It must be Tim. He walks over to the front door as Tim approaches.

"What is going on here you two," he says, condescendingly.

I look over at Brian, waiting for him to explain the mess we're in now. As usual, he says nothing.

"Well, we were at a party at Marcus and Janet's house and we got into a fight when we got home and Brian punched a hole in our bedroom wall and then he broke a chair," I say as I point to Exhibit B in the kitchen. "And now he just called the cops on himself."

Tim looks at him, then back at me.

"I didn't think that we should be alone together tonight so I thought if you came over that you could either stay here or take one of us home with you," I tell him.

"OK, well, let's go then," and he looks over at Brian.

"I can't now," Brian says. "The County is on their way here and if I leave I'll be fleeing a police officer."

"Well, what if we all go?" I say. "If we all go then nobody will be home."

They look at each other. I feel brilliant in my drunken stupor. But it's too late. Brian's head turns first and then we all look to the east and see the first flashing red lights of the law heading toward our house, followed by three other sets of lights. We watch as they come closer and then the first squad car flies past the field drive but then turns around on the road that Marcus and Janet live on. The second squad car slows and turns into our drive, followed by the third car, then the last. In seconds, there are 2 police officers standing on our front porch, followed by two others shortly thereafter. I am sitting on the couch now, trying to decide what I am going to say. Brian opens the door, and they step inside.

"Evening, officer," Brian says, slurring.

Tim steps in to try to save the day, once again.

"Officer," he says, addressing the taller of the two. "I think there's been a misunderstanding. We've got things under control now. These two have been drinking and they were fighting but everything is fine now. I'm going to take Brian with me so there aren't any more problems."

The officer explains the standard policy again. That when they receive a domestic dispute complaint, that they have to investigate and remove one member of the household. Brian looks at me, irritated, as if it's my fault. The officer explains that they are going to interview all of us separately, starting with Brian.

"First of all, let's see this hole in the wall," one officer says, almost chuckling under his breath.

"Can you show us where it is?" another says to Brian.

Brian turns toward the hallway to our bedroom and Tim starts to follow.

"No," the officer says. "I'd like you to stay here with Erika while we interview Brian."

Tim looks at him and then at Brian. They continue down the hallway and Tim goes to the kitchen to look at the chair. After a few minutes, another officer comes to the front door, knocks and lets himself in.

He nods at me and looks around. Another officer comes out from the bedroom and they exchange some details about the evening.

"Apparently, the husband called 911 after he punched the hole in the wall and broke one of the kitchen chairs," he says.

"Ma'am," he turns to address me. "Did he put his hands on you at all?"

"He just grabbed me on the arms, that's all. I wasn't the one who called 911, Brian was. And I told the dispatcher that I didn't want them to send anyone out here, but the dispatcher said that they had to," I tell them.

"Just a minute, ma'am. We're going to get your testimony in just a minute," he says.

Since I'm not supposed to say anything more, I sit there, just staring at them, angry at this whole situation and wanting them to get the fuck out of our house. Then, one of the officers pulls out his tape recorder, presses some buttons, and then starts asking me questions about what happened earlier in the night. Tim is standing there, listening to me.

I remember being surprised that they would let him stand there and listen, thinking that it probably should have been confidential. A few minutes later, Brian comes out from our bedroom with the other two officers. He stares at me again. I look away. The officer who appears to be the lead steps toward Brian.

"Well, given the circumstances, we're going to have to arrest you for domestic assault," the officer says.

"Please don't," I say. "I was not even the one who called 911. He was. I really do not want him to be arrested. I will not be pressing charges."

The officers say nothing, probably either thinking that I'm stupid or he's one damn lucky man to have a wife like me. One of them puts his hand on the back of Brian's shoulder and pushes him toward the door. I stand up, looking at him, for forgiveness or understanding or complacency. As they escort him out the door, I am crying. I can't even recall how we got to this point; little moments of time that spiraled out of control.

"Please don't," I say again.

The officer who interviewed me tells them that since tomorrow is New Year's Day that Brian will have to spend two nights in jail because they won't have his pre-trial hearing until Tuesday morning. I watch as they walk him around the corner of the house toward the squad car. A few minutes later, all three cars head down the driveway. At the field drive, one car heads west. The other two, and the one with Brian in it, head east. I am sitting on the couch then, my head in my hands, and Tim is staring at me. It's 2:30 in the morning.

"What am I going to tell the kids tomorrow?" I ask him.

"Just tell them the truth," he says.

"Tell them that their Dad is in jail?" I say, crying.

"Yes, tell them that you got into a fight, and that Brian got very angry, and that he couldn't control his temper," he says.

I cannot even fathom saying that to my kids, but I don't want to lie to them either, especially Bryce.

"I don't know," I tell him. "I just need to get some sleep. I'll be over early in the morning to get them, OK?"

"OK, good night," he says, as he gives me a hug.

He walks out with the pieces of the kitchen chair, like all he has to do is glue them back together and everything will be fine.

Chapter 21

The next morning I wake up looking at the hole in our bedroom wall. I start crying and it's only 7:30. My face is swollen and red from all of the emotions from the night before. I call my parents to see if they will pick up the kids and bring them home. I don't want to face Brian's parents right now. My Dad answers the phone.

"Hey Dad," I say. "I was just wondering if you would go get the kids at Tim and Marilyn's house."

"Well, what are you doing that you can't go get them?" he asks me, since I'm a grown adult and they're my kids.

"Well, I don't know how to tell you this, but Brian and I got into a fight last night after we got home from the party at Marcus and Janet's house, and he ended up punching a hole in the wall and he broke a kitchen chair, and then he called the cops on himself, basically," I say, matter of factly. "So they came, and they interviewed us, and then they took him to jail. And he'll have to be there until tomorrow."

My Dad just says nothing at all for a moment. I cannot even imagine what is going through his mind. I am his baby girl and he probably just wants to kick Brian's ass.

He takes a deep breath, then says, "OK, we'll go get the kids and bring them home then. See you in a bit."

About an hour later my parents show up at our house with the kids. Bryce looks at me and immediately knows something is wrong.

I suppose it's the tears in my eyes, or the way that I can't look at him for more than a few seconds. He comes over and hugs me and I start crying.

"What's wrong, mom?" he asks, the voice of a 12-year-old but mature beyond his years.

I don't say anything. Bennett walks into the living room and looks around.

"Where is Dad," he asks?

I tell him to come over to me, grabbing his hand to have him sit down. Bryce sits down on the couch next to me. Bennett is on my lap.

My mom is holding Becca.

"I have to tell you guys something," I say. "Last night your Dad and I got into a big fight and he got really, really angry at me. He punched a hole in the wall in our bedroom and broke a chair. And the police came and they had to take him to jail."

I look at Bryce. His eyes are full of tears and now mine are too. My mom is crying too.

Bennett asks in an innocent voice, "Well what were you fighting about?"

"We were just fighting about something that happened at Marcus and Janet's party," I tell them, reaching for answers that will fit both their ages.

"Well, why did Dad get so mad?" Bennett asks.

"Well, we were drinking and we were both mad and he just got really angry. Then he called the cops and they had to take him to jail,"

I say.

Then Bennett gets up from the couch and walks toward his bedroom. Apparently, he's had enough of this. I want to say, me too.

Bryce has still said nothing.

"When will he be able to come home so we can be a family again,"

Bryce finally asks in a broken voice, still fighting back breaking down.

"Hopefully tomorrow," I tell him.

And then he starts sobbing. I go over to him and put my arm around him, pulling him closer to me. His legs and shoulders are shaking. After a few minutes, he looks relieved, like he's glad that he doesn't have to tell his friends that his Dad can't come to his basketball game next weekend because he's spending a little time in the clinker.

I look over at Becca. She is only 4 but I know that she understands everything that we just said. She is watching Bryce crying and then she starts. I feel like my heart is breaking. I pray to God she will not remember this. She buries her face into my mom's chest, and I want to be the one holding her. My parents are both looking at me. I feel like they are proud of how I handled this. They stay with us for a little while as things smooth over, and then I am home alone with my kids, wondering how I can wish away the night before.

I wait all day for a call from Brian. I think about the movies where the inmate gets one call to anywhere and I wonder if I will be that person for him. I wonder what color suit he is wearing, or if he just gets to stay in his own clothes. I don't want to go anywhere. I don't want to be seen in public. Once the word gets out that there were cop cars in our driveway, I know that people will be talking about this for weeks.

My arms hurt from where Brian was grabbing me. I'll probably have to wear long sleeve shirts for as long as the gossip goes on. My voice is almost gone from yelling at him. My throat is sore. I wait until around 4 o'clock before I decide to call the jail. I spend 15 minutes trying to figure out which number it might be in the phone book, and just about decide to give up. Obviously I am not the one person that he decided to call when he had the chance. I'm pissed off and hurt. I decide to start with the dispatch center. They refer me to the "inmate coordinator."

I decide of all the jobs in the world, I would probably not want that one.

A woman answers the phone.

"Hi," I say. "My name is Erika Daniels and my husband was arrested last night for a domestic dispute. His name is Brian Daniels."

I pause. I'm assuming that she is looking at a list.

"Yeah," she says. "We've got him. He'll be in until Tuesday, since it's a holiday."

"Well, do you know what time he'll be able to leave?" I ask.

"Well, his pre-hearing is set for 9 a.m.," she informs me.

"Wait," I say. "What's the hearing for?"

"Well, under state laws, the state has to prosecute for domestic assault even if the victim chooses not to. So he'll see the judge on Tuesday morning and they'll decide if he has to post bail or can be released on his own recognizance," she tells me.

"OK, well do I need to be there for that?" I ask.

"That's up to you," she says. "The judge will probably want you there. He may keep your husband until he can talk more with you."

"OK, well thank you," I say as I hang up.

I seriously consider just leaving him in there for a few days so maybe he'll learn his lesson. Every part of me does not want to go to that hearing Tuesday, but I'll go anyway. Because for some unfathomable reason, he's my husband and I still love him.

The next day at the hearing, Brian's Dad is waiting outside the courtroom when I get there.

"Good morning," he says as I approach him.

"Good morning," I politely respond.

There is a gentlemen standing next to him that I have never seen before. He is very tall, thin, and balding, with a well-trimmed beard and mustache. He is wearing a charcoal-gray suit. Tim introduces him as Brian's lawyer. I shake his hand and force a smile. I am so mad that Brian did not include me in this conversation, and that I had no input on the direction that this was going to take. Then I realize that I did when I chose not to press charges against him. But to him I am still the enemy, because I am still the only one who has the choice.

When we get in the courtroom, Brian is escorted in by the bailiff.

He will not even look at me. His face is scruffy from not shaving and he has huge dark bags under his eyes. He looks so tired. Once he is seated, he stares straight ahead. The court is called into session. The judge asks if I am present and I respond that I am. He asks me to confirm that I do not want to press charges. He asks me if I believe Brian should be allowed to be at home. He asks me if I believe Brian should be released on his own recognizance. I tell him yes.

"I just want him to come home, so that we can be a family again," repeating what Bryce said to me the day before, my voice breaking.

The judge allows him to be released without posting bail. He will be transported back to the jail where he can get his things. His court date has been set for the middle of April. When I get to the jail, Brian's Dad is already there waiting for him. The security door opens and Brian walks out, looking briefly at me, almost through me, a cold, blank stare. He walks directly past me and out the door into freedom. Tim and I both follow him. I don't have any idea what to say. He stays close to his Dad and then turns in the direction of Tim's car. Mine is parked on the other side of the lot.

"Aren't you going home with me?" I ask, almost begging in my voice. I feel like I already know the answer but I ask anyway.

"No, Erika, I'm not going anywhere with you," he says.

I cannot believe it. I stop walking. I want to sit down on the sidewalk and cry. He is treating me like this is my fault, like I'm to blame for this whole situation. This is shameful and hurtful and irritating and embarrassing, and he's the stupid man who called the cops in the first place. All I can think about is what I am going to tell the kids when they get home from school and their Dad isn't there.

Later that afternoon, he shows up at our house, just after the kids get home from school. He ignores all of my attempts to talk to him, but spends time with the kids like he's a fucking martyr. I make dinner, take the kids to soccer and come back, then start getting them settled for bed. Finally after the kids are in bed that night, I go downstairs where he is watching TV.

"So why are you giving me the silent treatment?" I politely ask.

"I don't want to talk to you, Erika," he responds, looking over at me and then back at the TV.

Wow, well this is starting out well. I consider turning around and going back upstairs to save myself the pain and misery of the way he is about to treat me.

"Why?" I ask. "I don't understand. What did I do? You're the one who called 911 the other night. I didn't press charges on you, and I could have. I want us to try to work this out. I want us to try to turn this around. Don't ask me why. I guess I'm crazy."

I think back for a moment. I guess it's how I was raised. When I was growing up, if my parents were disagreeing about something, they wouldn't speak for days sometimes. My Dad would hole up in the shop that he had in our second garage and only come out to eat and sleep, then head back in to the trenches. My mom would cry, watch TV

all night by herself, and then after a few days of the cycle, she would go a little crazy and start yelling until she felt better. It was totally dysfunctional. And no matter how much we don't want to become our parents, it seems impossible to avoid. For Brian and me, he is the one who avoids conflict as much as possible, not necessarily giving into me, but just not arguing about them, as if his decision is the last word.

He refuses to even discuss things at times. I am the one who usually wants to confront things, talk about them, and move on. The affair with Shelley was just the one damn thing that I couldn't get over.

"I don't know, Erika," he says. "I'm just tired of going around and around about this. This all started with you going back to the whole Shelley thing."

"Really," I interrupt then, irritated. "Our fight on New Year's Eve started when you took Sara and gyrated your groin into her on Marcus and Janet's sink, remember?"

"Whatever, Erika," he shoots back. "You were going to fight with me about something that night. It was just a matter of time."

"Bullshit," I holler back. "I don't want to live like this either. We've been through so much shit and I'm tired of it too."

"Then why do you keep bringing it up," he asks. "Why do you keep going back?"

"Because I'm not over it, that's why. I'm trying. Remember when the counselor told us it could take 7 years for a spouse to get over an affair?" I remind him.

"I already told you, I am not waiting that long to move on with my life," he says, going back to watching TV and flipping through the channels.

"Good God, like you're the only one with a life here," I shriek. "Can you not have a 15-minute conversation without watching that God damn television?"

I get up to walk away.

"I'm done talking about this. I don't want to keep going back to the Shelley thing. We have to move on," he says.

"That's fine, you can be done all you want, but that doesn't mean it's over. You can't just make it go away because you want it to be," I tell him.

I turn away from him and start walking up the stairs. When I look up, Bryce is standing there watching me, tears streaming down his handsome little face.

Chapter 22

*T*he next few months are peculiar for a couple who is about to be divorced by the end of the year. We are on and off, hot then cold, sweet to sour. In January, my parents and I join Brian on a business trip to Phoenix. In February, the two of us head to Neuvo Vallarta for a few days. In March, we take the kids and my Dad to baseball spring training in Fort Myers. In the middle of April we travel to Laughlin with my parents, and aunt and uncle. For Mother's Day, Brian gives me a beautiful mother's bracelet with the birthstones of the kids. And then, on a whim, he decides to go out and buy a Harley Davidson motorcycle.

On Cinco de Mayo of that year, we spend the day at the kids' soccer games. We don't make other plans, assuming that Marcus and Janet will be having their annual fiesta. When we don't hear from them by mid-afternoon, Brian decides to call Marcus to see what they are up to.

"Hey Marc," he says into his cell phone. "You guys have plans tonight?"

There's a pause.

"Oh ok," he says, sounding disappointed. I look over at him and his face shows the same. He listens for a little bit longer.

"OK, well, let us know if you change your mind," he says. "We're going to be home, just hanging out with the kids, so you can come over here or we can come there too. Whatever, just let us know. Yeah, bye."

"Well, that's weird," I say. "I wonder why they aren't having friends over for Cinco de Mayo?"

"No idea," Brian says, annoyed with something, probably me.

We stop and get ice cream cones on our way, and then head home to spend the evening with the kids.

Early the next morning, we get a call from the woman who lives just down the road from Marcus and Janet. I answer the phone.

"Hi there," she says, pausing. "Is this Erika?"

"Yes," I say, intrigued a little by the older woman's voice on the other end of the line.

"Erika, this is Margaret Johnson," she says, with a slight Scandanavian accent, "Marcus and Janet's neighbor."

"Oh, hi Margaret," I say. "How are you? Are you surviving all this rain we've been having?"

"Oh yes, I'm just fine," she says.

Margaret is a woman who lives about 500 yards from Marcus and Janet's house, as the crow flies. She is probably in her early to mid-80s, a friendly woman in public but someone who keeps to herself otherwise.

Her husband died back in the '60s. She raised her three kids alone and has lived in the same old 3-bedroom farmhouse since she married. A bit lonely, she spends a lot of time at Marcus and Janet's house, most of the time with Marcus. They garden and drink beer together, and Marcus helps her with odd jobs to keep up her property.

A little puzzled, I say, "So what's going on with you today?"

"Well, I'm just a little worried about my neighbors over here. There were three county sheriff cars that pulled into their driveway early this morning around 2 a.m. So I called over there a few times then to see if everything was alright," she says. "The lights were on but nobody answers, not even now."

"Hmm, well, that's strange," I say, feeling like she might be a bit on the nosy side.

"And then around 6:30, a little light-colored car pulled in the driveway, and a man got out of the car," she mutters. "About 15 minutes later, Janet and the girls came out of the house, got in the car and left."

"Hmm, well that's weird," I say again.

Turning to Brian, I ask "Have you talked to Marcus since last night?"

"No," he says. "But he said they were just going to stay home last night."

I relay the story that Margaret just shared with me. She is listening in the background. Brian grabs his cell phone off the counter and dials Marcus' number. No answer.

Then, she says, "Well, I just wondered if maybe you guys want to try to call them. They might think I'm just being nosy or something, but they might answer if you call."

"Sure, we can do that," I confirm. "We'll try getting a hold of them.

Thanks for letting us know."

"I don't want to make something out of nothing, but I just want to make sure everything is OK over there," she says.

"Yep, nope, we'll give'em a call," I say again. "Thanks."

When I hang up the phone, Brian has a strange look on his face. He calls Marcus, with no answer again. I go back to the bedroom and grab my phone to call Janet. She answers.

"Hi there," she says, her voice quiet, flat.

"What's going on?" I ask.

"What do you mean?" she responds back.

"Well, we just got a call from Margaret, and she said that there were three sheriff cars in your yard early this morning. Then later she saw you and the girls leave in a car around 7."

She sighs, her voice trembling, then she says, "I don't even know where to start."

She tells me that they had some people over for a little party last night for Cinco de Mayo. A pit starts forming in my stomach, wondering why we weren't invited. She says that Marcus got really drunk and that she wanted him to sleep on the couch downstairs instead of in bed with her, but he didn't want to. He got really angry and she locked herself in their bedroom with Amy because she was scared of him.

She told me Jenna was already sleeping downstairs. For a moment, I go back to December. I know exactly what she is talking about. I am quiet, just listening, but afraid for her. She tells me that Marcus was trying to break down the door, trying to get to her and Amy. He was pounding on the door, screaming for her to let him in for 45 minutes.

Finally she called the cops. By the time they got to their house, Marcus was nowhere to be found. They looked all over the house, then outside in the garage, and then walked into the woods. It was dark and they had flashlights, but they didn't find him. The officers told her that she should leave the house until they could locate them, so she called her brother to come get her and the girls, and that's where she was when I called her.

It takes me back to the night that Brian left with Shelley, that feeling of not wanting to believe he really left. For a moment, I am back there, in that night, frantically searching the house for my husband with Janet.

"Oh my God. I'm so sorry, Janet," I say. "What can I do?"

Brian is watching me, his face concerned.

"Nothing right now," she says. "They only have so many hours to find him before the warrant runs out and then they can't arrest him.

I'm not going back there. I'm leaving him, Erika. I can't live this way with my kids. He was so drunk last night. Amy was crying, terrified. I don't want her to be afraid of her own Dad."

Suddenly, Brian's phone is ringing and I can tell by the way that he is talking that it's Marcus on the other end. I don't say anything for a moment. I want to put the story on pause, like it's a movie that I'm watching and I can just hit the button on the remote before it spins crazy, out of control.

"I don't know what to say," I admit to her. "I know what it feels like."

"I know you do. I just can't go back there," she says. "I'm going to live with my parents for a little while, until I can find a place of my own.

But he's not going to make it easy for me to leave."

"You're right," I confirm. "Well, let me know if there's anything we can do, help you find a place or help you move, or take the girls, whatever it is, just let me know. You can always stay here too, if you need to."

"OK," she says. "Thank you so much, Erika. I really appreciate it."

"You're welcome," I tell her.

"Oh, and one more thing," she says. "Can you please not tell anyone what is going on? I don't want to have to deal with the questions and gossip until I can figure out what I'm going to do."

"Sure," I say. "I understand. Take care, and call me when you need something, OK?"

"Yes, I will. Bye."

Brian is still talking to Marcus when I hang up. I'm listening to him, trying to piece together what happened. He tells Marcus that they should get together for a beer that week, to talk. They have been friends since they were kids and I hope that Marcus will confide in him like he has in the past, even though their friendship has changed over the past few months.

"What in the hell is going on," I say, after he hangs up his phone.

"I don't know," Brian says. "Marcus says he was just really drunk and he just wanted Janet to open the door."

"Good grief," I say. "She says she's going to leave him. It's not like they haven't had their share of problems, but this seems kind of sudden, don't you think?"

"I don't know," he says. "I guess she's just had enough."

"Yeah, I guess so," I say, standing there a moment looking at Brian.

I realize this is going to turn our lives upside down. More than I ever know.

Janet calls a few days later and asks if she can come over. The girls are going to spend some time with Marcus that evening and she wants to just come and hang out, sync music and have a beer. When she gets to our house, we all greet her at the door. We haven't told the kids anything about what is going on with them, so they are confused when she arrives without the girls.

"Hey there, lady," I say, giving her a big hug and holding it. She tries to let go like she doesn't need it, but I just hold on. When I finally let her go, she has tears in her eyes.

"Hi," she says, smiling through her tears. The kids look at me, puzzled.

"Where are the girls," Bennett asks first.

"They are home . . . um, they are with Marcus tonight," she says, realizing that soon it will be his house and it won't be home for her anymore.

Janet and I stroll to the kitchen. The boys head back to the basement, and Brian goes to finish up some work on his computer in the nook.

"Whattya want to drink?" I ask, heading to the fridge. "We've got beer or wine, or I've got some mixed margaritas too."

"Oh, a margarita sounds great," she says.

Her face is shallow, tired, expressionless. Her eyes are red, like the night she spent with me when Brian left with Shelley.

I start mixing our drinks: salt on the rim, ice, on the rocks. I hand Janet her margarita and she holds it up for us to cheers.

"Here's to you, here's to me, the best of friends we'll always be, and if we ever disagree, the fuck with you, and here's to me," I say with a wink and a smile as our glasses meet. It's her favorite toast of mine.

It's the least I can do right now.

"So did you bring your thing to download music?" I ask. "We've got quite a variety of stuff, from country to alternative, a little bit of pop, some rap. Whattya want?"

"Well, I've been running to help with the stress so I just wanted some new music. I'm getting tired of the old stuff," she says.

Brian is done at the computer, so I walk over and sit down. I load our music and start throwing out names of songs and bands. She hands me her player and I connect it.

"You have to hear this new song by Taylor Swift. Stacy played it for me when I was at her house the other night," she says.

Oh, no, I don't. I don't like Stacy. I think she's a conniving little bitch, kind of like what Shelley was for me. Except I'm pretty sure Stacy's in love with Janet, not Marcus. Hearing her name reminds me of New Year's Eve, watching her whisper in Brian's ear from across the room.

"What's the name of it," I ask. "What's it about?"

"It's called 'White Horse,' she tells me. "It's kind of hard to explain what it's about, but I have it on my player if you want to hear it."

She walks over to me and points at the song on the screen, and I play it.

I'm not a princess, this ain't a fairytale I'm not the one you'll sweep off her feet and lead her up the stairwell.

This isn't Hollywood, this is a small town.

I was a dreamer before you came and let me down.

Now it's too late for you and your white horse, to come around.

When the song finishes, she is wiping away tears.

"Do you like it?" she asks, her voice trembling.

"Yes, I like it," I tell her. "I love it, actually. Let's hear it again."

We listen to the song again. Five more times, in fact. I feel like it's me. I feel like it's Janet. And every woman like us who let a man interrupt her dreams.

Chapter 23

The next week, I get invited to go on a bus trip with a bunch of ladies. It just happens to be the same weekend of Brian's annual fishing trip. I want to go since I rarely get invited on trips like that, so I ask Brian's mom to keep the kids so I can go. It is a bar hopping sort of trip. By the time that we get to the bar at the end of the night, I am wasted. When I walk in the door, the first person I see is Cole. I look around the bar for Shelley, but I don't see her anywhere. I have never had the chance to be alone with him and talk about what happened.

I walk over to say hello. He is sitting with his brother, Justin, who is a nice little piece of eye candy too.

"I haven't seen you in forever. How have you been?" I ask.

"Good. How 'bout you?" he says.

"I'm wasted," I admit.

He laughs and flashes me his killer smile. Damn, I forgot how hot he is. He tells me it's his birthday so I buy him a drink. We chat for a few more minutes and then I go to the bathroom. When I come back, he is heading toward the door to leave. I figure this is my chance to talk to him, to apologize, to hear his side of the story, to tell him mine. And if I didn't right at that very moment, I may not have the chance again. I follow him outside.

"Cole," I yell after him.

He stops in the middle of the street. I walk to meet him there. I am shivering, not because it is cold but because I am nervous.

"What are you doing, drunky drunk?" he asks me, smiling again.

"I feel like we need to talk, Cole," I say.

"About what?" he asks. His face gets serious.

"Everything," I say, for lack of knowing how to describe what's on my mind. "I've hardly seen you and it's been almost two years."

He turns around and heads toward his truck.

"Will you give me a ride home?" I ask, trying to not sound desperate.

"I don't know if that's such a good idea," he says.

"Why not," I ask.

"Well, I'm trying to work things out with Shelley," he tells me.

"And I'm trying to work things out too," I say. "Nothing is going to happen. Trust me."

"I do trust you," he confirms. "What do you want to know?"

"I just want to know what you know," I say.

"OK," he says. "Get in."

I open the door, but before I can get in, he has to move a bunch of shit in the front seat. A jacket and his youngest son's car seat, a diaper bag on the floor. It reminds me how much I miss seeing his boys. He starts the truck and we head out of town.

"So tell me everything," I say again.

"Well, what do you want to know?" he asks. I'm growing tired of the cat and mouse game.

"Did they fuck?" I ask.

He turns and looks at me with his beautiful dark brown eyes like he is begging me not to make him say it to me. He shakes his head. Then he hits the steering wheel with his hand.

"I knew he never fucking told you! I knew that if he really told you the truth that you wouldn't still be with him, that you would have left him a long damn time ago," he says.

My eyes fill with tears. I cannot believe this is happening. Two fucking years, two years of my life wasted because Brian did not have the balls to tell me the truth. It was the truth all this time. I knew it in my heart, but I couldn't justify leaving him if he never admitted it to me. Somehow I thought he at least loved me enough to say it to my face. I said nothing.

"I'm sorry, Erika," he says. "I'm sorry that I had to be the one to tell you."

"It's OK," I say. "Someone had to tell me sooner or later."

We sit in silence for a few minutes. I know he feels bad that I know the truth.

"So how long have you known?" I ask.

"Well, Shelley didn't tell me right away either," he says. "It was about two months later that she finally told me."

"So what did she tell you?" I ask.

"She told me that after we left the bar that night, that she got a text from Brian asking her to come pick him up at your house. I was already asleep and her mom was there with the kids," he says.

"Did her mom ever tell you that I called your house that night, looking for them?" I ask.

"You did?" he asks. "No, she never told me. God, what a bitch, in my own house," and he pauses. "So, anyway, she went to your house and you were gone somewhere with Janet. She said they were sitting in the car, just talking, when you pulled in the driveway. Brian told her they should go for a drive so that's when they left and passed you in the driveway. She said they just drove around for a while and listened to music, and then they went out to the State Park, and that's where it happened."

"You mean they fucked at the State Park?" I ask, reluctant to know the answer because it will ruin all memories I have of that place.

"Yeah, in the front seat of the car," he says.

"Oh my God," I say. "No way."

An image of my tall, stocky husband fucking Shelley in the front seat of her little sedan comes to my mind and I can't help but smile.

What a couple of idiots.

"After that, she drove him home and he told her to drop him off by the field drive and he would walk up the driveway to the house," he tells me.

"And that's it?" I ask.

"Well, she told me that they talked for a few days after that, but it never happened again," he says.

"Do you believe her?" I ask.

"I have to, don't I?" he replies.

I don't know what to say. I hate her so badly for what she's done.

But I know I can't make Cole hate her. In spite of everything, I know that he still loves her.

"I know you don't want to hear this, but I hate your wife. I think she's a whore and a bitch. And I hate her for ruining my marriage," I tell him.

"And I hate Brian too," he admits. "I think he's a fucking asshole."

I guess it should have hurt me when he said it, but I completely understand. And I think he understands me too. By now we are sitting in his truck in front of our house, probably in the very same spot that Brian and Shelley sat parked and talking that night. We look at each other for a moment and then the whole conversation changes.

"So now what," he says.

"What do you mean?" I ask.

"Where're we gonna go from here?" he asks me.

"I don't know," I say. My eyes are glazed over. My mind is exhausted from this conversation.

"Can I have a hug?" he asks.

"Sure," I say.

He leans toward me across the seat. We could have kissed but I turn my head and just pull him into me. That's all I can handle at this moment. When I start moving away, he grabs my arms and holds me there.

"You're so beautiful, Erika. You don't even know how beautiful you are, on the inside, everything. I've wanted you my whole life," he tells me.

"Yeah, whatever," I say.

"No really," he says. "I mean it."

He is still holding me close to him.

"Well, this is not the time for us to be doing something like that. All the wrongs those two have done are not going to be made right by us sleeping together tonight. Not now," I tell him.

I pull away from him then. I know that all the vengeance I am feeling for my husband and Cole's wife are not going to be bettered by fucking him at that very moment, but God damn, did I ever want to.

What a lying, cheating son-of-a-bitch.

"Thanks for the ride," I say, as I get out of the truck. "Thanks for everything, Cole."

I wave as I round the corner of the house. I am thrilled that I finally know the truth.

By the time I get in the house, I am a hurricane. I slam the door behind me and throw my purse on the ground. It is quiet and cold in our house. Like everything is a lie. Like everything should be burned to the ground. I want to pack his shit up so it is ready when he gets home.

Better yet, forget the packing. I'd heard stories of women who just threw their husband's stuff on the front lawn. That sounds like a great idea. Perfect.

It is 2 a.m. I don't care. I dial Brian's cell phone number. If I am going to vent to anybody, it might as well be him. I never thought he would answer.

"Hellooo," I hear his drunk voice on the other end of the line.

"You lying, cheating, God-damn son-of-a-bitch," I say. "How could you lie to me all this time? How could you look me in the eye every fucking day for almost two fucking years and lie to me like that?" I ask, screeching into the phone.

"Erika, what are you talking about" he says, in a perfectly diplomatic tone. I can tell there are people around him.

"You and Shelley fucked," I say, like he's actually going to confirm it.

"What are you talking about?" he asks me. Now it is his liar's voice.

"Don't lie to me anymore, Brian. Just quit fucking lying to me. Tell me the truth," I say, trying to sound demanding.

"I told you the truth. I never fucked Shelley," he says.

"You're a god damn liar. I just got a ride home from Cole and he told me the whole story. Shelley told him everything," I say.

"Well, Shelley's lying then. I never fucked her," he says again.

"Oh OK, so you expect me to believe that she would lie to her husband about fucking you? For what reason, so she could be with you?" I ask.

"I have no idea why she would lie to him, Erika. How should I know?" he asks.

"Just quit fucking lying to me. Why can't you just tell me the truth?" I ask.

"I am telling you the truth," he says. "So what happened with you and Cole? Did you fuck him tonight then, you little whore?"

He's yelling back at me now. For once, I feel like he actually cares about what is happening. In the background, I can hear his Dad's voice.

But I'm infuriated that he's trying to turn this around on me again.

"Alright, that's enough," I hear his Dad say. "You need to talk about this when you're not drinking."

"You've got to be kidding me. You're going to try turning this around on me now?" I ask.

"I gotta go. We can talk about this when I get home tomorrow," he says, then hangs up on me.

"You might as well not even come home at all," I say, and I hang up the phone, bawling.

The next day, I feel like hell. In the morning I get the kids from Brian's mom and say as little as possible. I keep thinking about the night she told me it was my fault that this happened in the first place.

The kids and I hang out at home the rest of the day. When Brian gets home, the kids are all over him. It makes me sick how they can miss someone who is such a two-timing, lying, son-of-a-bitch. Later that night, we re-hash the same conversation we had over the phone. I tell him I just want to know the truth. He says he already told me the truth.

I tell him I want him to move out. He says he won't. Enough said. I sleep on the couch.

Chapter 24

*I*n the next couple of weeks, not only am I worried about what is happening with my marriage, but I am worried about what is going on with Marcus and Janet. I'm worried about the girls. Jenna, my goddaughter, and how this will change our relationship. I'm worried about my kids, trying to explain how people get divorced, just like that.

I'm worried about our friendships with them. I haven't talked to Janet since the day Margaret Johnson called us, but not because I haven't tried. I've sent her e-mails and get no response. I call her cell phone and leave voicemails that she doesn't answer. I send her text messages to try to get together. Finally, on their 10th wedding anniversary, she e-mails me and says that their divorce is going to be final any day now.

She says she is relieved and is ready to move on with her life as a single woman. I ask her to go for coffee sometime, and she wants to meet the following day. She says she'll e-mail me in the morning to let me know what time she can go.

The next day she e-mails me and wants to meet at 9:30 at the Starbucks in the skyway. Perfect, I miss my friend, and I want to tell her about what's been going on with me and Brian. I want to find out how she is doing with all of the changes in her life. She's already there when I arrive. Her face is colorless, somber, and her eyes are sad. She looks like she hasn't slept in days, maybe weeks. I get my coffee, watching her expressions as she sits there. As I approach her, she stands up, facing me.

"How are you?" I ask, leaning in to her to give her a hug.

"I'm ok," she says, her voice shaking, not convincing me.

We both sit down, next to each other, in nice comfy chairs. I feel like I could stay there all day long.

"So what is going on," I ask.

"It's over, Erika," she says, tears welling in her eyes. "The divorce should be final tomorrow."

"I don't know what to say. It all just happened so fast. How are the girls doing?" I wonder.

"I know. It went really fast. I submitted the papers online a couple of weeks ago," she says.

Wow, an online divorce. How strange, I'm thinking. How in the world do people accomplish a divorce online, I wonder, but then I realize that Marcus is still in love with her and he probably gave her everything she asked for.

"The girls are doing fine," she continues. "They are confused and they want to see Marcus more than what is possible right now, especially Jenna. You know, her and Marcus have always been close."

"So what are your plans?" I ask. "Where will you live, what's the custody going to be, all that stuff."

She takes a deep breath and looks sideways down the hallway of the skyway. For some reason, I get the feeling that she isn't telling me everything. I don't know why. She keeps looking down at her hands, which are trembling now. Her voice is still shaking.

"I'm actually closing on a townhome tonight, in SW, close to my parents. It's got 2 bedrooms and 2 baths, and it's perfect for me and the girls," she says, her eyes lighting up for a moment.

"Oh, that sounds perfect for you. And you won't have the maintenance of mowing and garbage and all that stuff. That will be good," I tell her.

"Yeah, I'm excited about it. We're going to have joint custody of the girls, a couple of days during the week and every other weekend. I want Marcus to have time with them too," she says.

"Well, I'm glad you're getting stuff figured out. I just want you to know that I'm your friend, regardless of what happens with you and Marcus, or Brian and Marcus. I'll be here for you. And I've been trying to get a hold of you but I'm sure you've been busy," I say.

"Yeah, I've been busy looking at townhouses, trying to keep the girls together, working on the petition. I just want it to be over," she says, looking relieved. Then, her face hardens again. "I just can't deal with his drinking anymore. I still love him, Erika. I feel like if I give him some time to get sober, to miss me and the girls, to be without us, that I could be with him again. I just can't be with him right now. And I'm not giving up on us forever, just for now."

"Do you really think he's capable of getting sober?" I question her.

"Yes, I really believe he can quit drinking," she answers. "But he has to do it on his own, because he wants to, because he wants us back, and because we're worth it to him. I've decided that I'll wait three years for him. After that, I'm moving on."

My heart hurts listening to her. I know what she's been through with him. It's lasted for years. And I'm angry at Marcus for putting her up to this, putting her through this hell. Janet doesn't deserve this.

Neither do the girls. I want to rail into him then, crucify him for what he's done. But then I soften because I know she loves him. I grab her hand and hold it.

She looks at our hands for a moment, then she picks her head up and says, "OK, so enough about me. What's going on with you guys?"

"Weellll, you should hear about what's going on with us," I say.

I lower my voice and tell her the long version of the story about the night with Cole.

"What are you going to do," she asks.

"I don't know. I still love Brian, but I just don't know if I can forgive this. I mean, how could he look me in the eye and lie to me every day for 2 years. Who does something like that?" I say.

She looks at me and just shakes her head, but says nothing. Tears are glassing her eyes again. She looks at her watch. We've been sitting there an hour.

"Well, I should get back to work," she says.

She stands up. I do too. We start walking back toward our office buildings, across the skyway and the busy street below. When we get close to where I have to turn off and part with her, I turn and lean in to give her another hug.

"OK, well, take care of yourself," I tell her. "I'll be thinking of you.

And please let me know if you need anything, help moving, keeping the girls, margaritas, whatever. I want to be here for you, ok?" I say, smiling.

"OK, I will," she says. "Talk to you soon."

And I watch her as she shakes her hot little bootie and her heels click clack on the tile floor. Stupid boy.

Chapter 25

*I*n the middle of June, on Father's Day, Brian comes home after celebrating with his parents and tells me that he wants a separation, a perfect present to himself. I already bought him a Harley jacket to match his new motorcycle. At this point, the only thing stopping me from wanting the separation too is my kids. I do not want them to grow up in a divorced family. But on the other hand, I don't want them growing up in dysfunction either. I want this to be a temporary situation until Brian and I can have some time apart. I wish that I had known then, that it wasn't the same for him. He was already emotionally gone.

At work, I am a mess. I fall apart, crying everywhere I go. I can't focus on anything. I decide to ask for some time off, to sort things out, figure out what I want to do. My manager is gone on vacation so I go to our director to explain what is going on. He tells me that he is sorry to hear about my situation, that I can take whatever time that I need, that I can come back whenever I am ready.

Brian and I decide that we will rotate every couple of days with the kids, and whoever has them will stay at the house so that their lives are disrupted as little as possible. I will have them on Mondays and Tuesdays. Brian will have them on Wednesdays and Thursdays. Then we will rotate every other weekend. I am happy that it's Monday and I get to be the one to stay for the first time. I finally get to see him leave, like he should have done so long ago.

"I want you to be the one to tell them," I tell him when we get home from work.

"Why, Erika, so I look like the bad guy?" he asks.

"Well, you are, aren't you?" I say.

"God, you're a bitch," he says.

"I know, Brian. You've been telling me that for 15 years, remember? I've started to believe it now."

We decide that we will tell the kids tonight and then Brian will be leaving. I ask him where he is going to stay, and he tells me that it's none of my business.

The kids spent that Monday with Brian's parents. His mom brings them home. Brian is back in the bedroom when they get there.

"So when do you want to tell the kids?" I ask.

He grabs an overnight bag out of the closet, already making plans to pack.

"Well, we might as well do it right now," he says.

"OK, let's go then. But I'm not going to be the one to tell them," I remind him again.

He looks at me, annoyed.

"That's just like you to make me do this alone when you want it just as much as I do," he says.

"Oh no, I don't," I admit. It hurts to say it.

"Whatever," he says, and turns away.

I walk out to the living room. I holler for the kids to come out there.

Becca is the first to get there, and I pick her up and hold her. The boys come up from the basement.

"Your Dad and I have something to tell you," I say.

Bryce's face is already somber. He is very observant, intelligent, and sensitive. I've got tears in my eyes. Brian stalls. Come on, already, just say it, I'm thinking. Tell them what you want, that you don't want to be with me anymore, that you're calling it quits to a marriage that you said you would never leave. I look at him, waiting for the truth to come.

"Your mom and I have decided that we're going to live separately for a while," he tells them.

"Why?" Bennett asks, looking at me for the answer.

"Because we need some time apart so we can sort through some things, and we think it will be better if we live apart," Brian says.

"Well, where are we going to go?" he asks.

"You're going to stay here, and your mom and I are going to live somewhere else when we're not here with you," he says.

I keep looking at each of them, waiting for the reality to set in.

I know that Bryce will be the first to acknowledge it, and the other two will follow him, however he chooses to react. For now, he is quiet.

I think about little moments with each them. Bryce, at preschool screening, when asked if he can hop on one foot, telling the teacher that he can't. She asks him if he will try, and he says he will, but he already knows he can't do it. Such a good sport. And Bennett, on his first birthday and already walking for 3 months, reaching out his arms to his grandma standing at the bottom of the steps while he falls head first down to the hard wood floor. The first of many goose eggs and bruises for him. And Becca, our little baby girl. When I woke up after having an emergency C-section with her, Brian is holding my hand and his tears are rolling down the side my face. All he ever wanted was a little girl. Wonderful moments of them, and now this shitty moment to file in my memory.

"Well, where are you going to live," Bennett asks, turning to me.

"I don't know yet, buddy," I say. "But I'll get it figured out."

"You could go to grandma and grandpa's house," he offers.

"I know I can, buddy, but I would kind of like a place where I can have some time to myself," I tell him.

He just looks at me, not really understanding why.

"I'll figure it out, OK? Don't you worry about it," I tell him, grabbing his hand, hoping he'll believe me.

But I know he will worry. This is just the first of many worries that my kids will have as their mom starts a new life on her own.

Before Wednesday, I've got to figure out where I am going to stay when I'm not at home with the kids. I remember that my cousin has a house in town that is sitting empty because she's living away at college for the summer. I call her mom to get her phone number. I'm sure she thinks it's strange, but I say nothing about what is going on.

I send her a text her if I can stay in the house for a little a while. I don't want to stay at my parents. And I feel like I've already outstayed my welcome at Kevin and Susan's house.

> Hey it's Erika. Do you think I could stay at your house for a few weeks?

> Sure, but what's going on?

Brian and I are separating and I need a place to stay when I don't have the kids

> Someone is going to be renting it starting July 1, but you can stay there until then.

How much do you want?

> Nothing. Don't worry about it.

There is nothing in there, no furniture.

> That's OK, I just need a place to crash. I have an air mattress I can use.

You can get the keys from my mom and Dad.

> I need them before Wednesday.

Just call them and they will get you some.

> Thank you!

No problem, lady!

I am thrilled that I have somewhere to go that I can be alone and that I don't have to live with my parents. I am hoping that two weeks will be enough time for us to be separated and figure things out. And somehow I'm still in denial that this is not the beginning of the end.

On Wednesday morning, I pack my stuff for the next couple of days. Since I'm not working, I decide that I'm going to golf like it's my job. I head to the course and spend the whole day there. Golf is one of those things that clears my head, helps me balance my perspective, gives me comfort. It reminds me of the times that I spent there as a young girl with my Dad, just golfing, saying nothing at all most of the time and enjoying some peace and quiet. For the first time in years, I decide to buy a season pass. And I'm going to buy some new golf clubs to replace the ones I've been using since high school. And dammit, I'm going to buy some fancy new golf shoes too. Like spending all that money is going to fix whatever problems I've got going on at home.

But I don't know that yet, and I'm still willing to try to see if it works.

Chapter 26

The first night in my cousin's house, I sleep like a champ, probably because of all of the beers that I had after volleyball that night.

But I know that not every night will be like the first one, unless I keep drinking. That's what I do a lot of the summer. I'm not ready to deal with any of this. I know that I need to stay strong for my kids, until we can get through mediation and start moving forward with the divorce. I stay there just a couple of weeks, but then, starting July 1, I have to find somewhere else to live. Another cousin Alicia just bought a house in a town nearby and says that I can stay with her if I need to.

Since I've got an air mattress, I can pretty much sleep anywhere as long as I have a roof over my head. I decide to stay with her during the month of July, and then look for a house to rent.

The following week, I start looking for a house, until I can decide what I want to do beyond that, until I have money for a down payment so I can buy something on my own. My friend who is a realtor takes me to see a house in town that is for rent until it can be sold. It's a beautiful, old Victorian-style house, and I fall in love with it the first time I see it. Literally, the moment I step inside, I love it. The kitchen has been remodeled in cherry cabinetry and Brazilian hardwood floors, but the rest of the house has the old woodwork and floors, even wallpaper in some rooms. There are enough bedrooms for the kids, and a huge open attic that would be fun to remodel into another bedroom or media area someday. It feels good to dream a little again. My life has been in limbo for so long.

"I love it! I think this will be perfect. When can I move in?" I ask.

"Well, the current owner is going through a divorce and wants to sell. The couple that is renting it now is going to be moving out next week to be closer to family, so really you can probably move in as soon as next weekend if you want to," she says.

It feels just right, like it was meant to be.

"I'll take it," I say. "Let me know how much I'll need for a deposit, and how soon I can move in. I'd like to bring the kids here in the next couple of days too."

When I leave, I immediately head to my parents' house to tell them.

I'm so excited about it that I want to tell them right away. I'm there for 3 minutes and my Dad is grilling me with questions. What about this, and what about that. How much will it be to heat it in the winter? What are you going to do if the house sells? Where will you live then?

I don't have any of the answers. Now I am frustrated. I wish that they could just be happy for a little while. I just know I don't want to live out of a bag any longer. For the first time in my life, I am going to be a single woman living alone, taking care of a house and a yard and three kids. Suddenly I'm scared to death.

It is Brian's weekend to have the kids. It works out nicely because I can stay at the house for the weekend because they are going camping with his parents. For the first time it will be without me. I want to see the kids before they leave so I rush home from work that afternoon.

Brian is picking them up today because they spent the day with his parents. When they get there, I tell Brian that I'd like to talk to him before they leave.

"What do you want to talk about? I'm kind of in a hurry. I want to get on the road so we don't have to deal with traffic," he says, trying to put me off.

"I found a house in town that I'm going to rent, starting next weekend," I tell him.

I figure he'll want to know where it is, what kind of house it is, how much the rent is going to be. At least considering that his kids will be living there with me.

"OK, sounds good. Is that what you wanted to talk about?" he asks.

"Yes," I say, feeling dejected. I guess he could care less.

"Well, I've been wanting to talk to you about something too," he says.

"What's that?" I ask, not really knowing that I'm just about to take a major blow to the ego.

"I've been thinking about the last few days and I've decided that I want a divorce," he tells me.

My heart falls in my chest. I don't know what to say. The kids are waiting out in the car to go camping for the weekend and he chooses right now to deliver me the news that he wants out of our marriage.

"Brian, please don't," I say.

"Don't what?" he says.

"Please don't leave me," I tell him.

"Erika, don't. I don't want to do this anymore. This is my chance, a second chance to move on with my life, and I'm going to take it. I want a divorce," he tells me.

I step toward him, but he starts walking down the hallway away from me, toward the mudroom.

"That's it?" I ask. "There's nothing more to talk about?"

"No, it's over. I don't want to be married to you anymore," he says.

"Well, you're going to have to file the paperwork. I'm not going to do it," I tell him.

"What do you mean, you won't sign it?" he says, irritation in his voice.

"No, I'll sign it, but I'm not drawing the papers and I'm not paying for it. You're going to have to do everything. I don't want a divorce,"

I tell him.

I'm tired of feeling like all I am is a pain in the ass to him. It hurts like hell. After all this, I wanted to be the one to say it was the end.

I wanted to be the one to kick him out in some dramatic moment. I guess I just wanted to be in control. I am crying then, not for sympathy, but because I realize that all summer all this has been for him was a way to let me down easy. I wonder how long it will take him to be fucking

Shelley or some other desperate housewife. He turns around and walks out the door to the garage. I walk to the garage and smile and wave at the kids as he backs out. They are waving and smiling back at me, none of us having any idea that the selfish son-of-a-bitch is about to break the news to them that their parents are getting a divorce, and he's going to do it without me.

When they're gone, I go hysterical. I am frantic, scared out of my mind, no idea what I am going to do, running around the house in a panic. It's not that I am afraid of being alone, at least right now. I'm afraid of being alone forever. I'm afraid that no one will ever love me again. Not that Brian ever did it well, but he tried. I know that I'm not the easiest person to live with. I've been mentally unstable, a bitch, a mess of low self-esteem. I'm more afraid of what this means for my kids. The label of them being from a divorced family, the stigmas that will follow them all their lives, at school, at church, when they go to college, get married, the rest of their damn lives. And I'll never be able to fix it or change it or make it better. I am so angry at him for giving up, at myself for not forgiving him, at Shelley for fucking my husband.

I text Brian.

When do you want to tell the kids?

I just did.

You are fucking kidding me?

No, you told me that you didn't want to be the one to tell them, and I didn't want to wait any longer, so I told them.

You are a son-of-a-bitch.

I text again.

I cannot believe you would do that without me.

And then again.

They will remember that the rest of their lives.

He texts nothing at all, which is really fine because there is nothing to say when a person has done something so incredibly selfish and wrong.

I spend the entire weekend at home, mostly in our bed. I feel like I am falling apart. My anxiety is high. My mood is low. Friends are texting me to get together and do something, but I feel like doing nothing at all. I feel like I am going backwards; going back to when we first moved into the new house, back to the time when I completely lost it.

Chapter 27

*I*t was March of 2004. Brian had just gotten his second DUI on New Year's Eve, with the babysitter in the car. We had moved into the new house in the country weeks before that, and Bennett's birthday was days away. I was in the middle of the enormous system replacement project at work. Besides having three kids, 2 dogs, a new house and a stressful job, I was overwhelmed by the idea that my husband was living his dream of a life in the country, and I wasn't so sure that I had the same dream.

It happened at work. I was in meetings all day long, a busy day, but nothing unusual. In fact, I actually got back to my desk around 3:30

which gave me some time to check some e-mails and wrap some things up before I left at 4. The only problem was that when I got back to my desk, I lost it. That's the best way I know how to explain it. I couldn't function. I couldn't think clearly. I felt completely incoherent, staring at my computer screen but not able to process anything that I was trying to read. My hands were shaking. I was sweating. My eyes were darting back and forth, unable to focus on anything for more than a few seconds. As I pushed back in my chair and quietly shut my office door, I was terrified that someone might see me in my office and stop by to chat. My hands felt numb. I was breathing faster and I felt like I couldn't slow it down. I wondered if I was having a heart attack, but my heart didn't really hurt either. I picked up the phone to call Brian.

Luckily he answered.

"Hey it's me," I said.

"Can I call you back?" he asked. "I'm on a call right now."

Normally, I would understand. Brian had a stressful job as a Software Engineer. He spent most of his days resolving technical computer problems for customers all over the world. He was one of the top guys at his company. He had a great reputation. He worked on fixing systems that were down or in critical situations, and there was no excuse for downtime for some of the companies that he supported.

"No, you can't," I said. "I need you."

"What's going on?" he asked.

"I don't know. I'm freaking out right now. I can't think straight. My hands are shaking. I feel like I'm losing my mind," I told him.

"Well, can you go home?" he asked.

"Yeah, but I don't know if I should drive," I told him.

"What do you mean?" he said.

"I don't know," I said, my voice breaking. "I'm scared. I don't know what's happening. I've never felt like this before."

"Well, if you can wait a little while I can come get you when I'm done with this call. But I don't know how long I'll be," he said.

"That's OK. I'm just going to go. I don't want to stay here anymore,"

I said.

"Well, call me if you need anything," he said.

I was in a fog but I got to my car and started driving home. I felt like was drunk, still incoherent, yet sober. About half way home, I realized I was supposed to get the kids. I was scared to be alone with them. I felt like I couldn't handle it. I called Brian again.

"Hi, it's me," I said.

"What, Erika?" he asked, annoyed.

"Would you mind picking up the kids after work? I just want to go home and go to bed," I told him.

"Yeah, I'll get them. And if I can't then I'll have my mom get them,"

he told me.

"No," I said. "If you can't then just call me and I will go back and get them."

"OK," he said. "Bye."

After that I missed three weeks of work and lost 20 pounds. Brian finally took me to the Emergency Room when I admitted that I was suicidal. Whatever was happening was scary enough to make me not want to live anymore. At the ER, they diagnosed me with panic attacks. The doctors offered me Ativan; an anti-anxiety drug that they explained can easily become addictive. I was worried that I would become addicted, but took it anyway; to get me through until the anti-depressant that they gave me kicked in.

A few days after I got home, I got a call from the Psychiatry Department at the hospital. They reviewed my record after my visit to the ER and they felt that I was a good candidate for something called Cognitive Behavioral Therapy (CBT). I had never heard of it but said I would give it a try. I felt hopeless, like I had nothing to lose. They told me that in 1 or 2 treatments they could usually turn around most patients with panic and anxiety disorders. I scheduled my appointment for early May, and regulated my doses of Ativan until then.

At the beginning of my therapy that day, the doctors asked me to identify all of the symptoms that I associated with my panic and anxiety. I had to complete 100-page questionnaire. When I was done, I was exhausted. For me, my key symptoms at that time were shortness of breath, sweating, shaking hands and racing thoughts. My panic had gotten so bad, that if I even had one of those physical symptoms, my body began its fight or flight response and tricked my mind into being afraid of the symptoms. As part of the CBT, the psychologists wanted me to bring on the symptoms that I feared so that I could train my gut and my brain that I don't need to be afraid of the symptoms. It scared the hell out of me, but I had nowhere else to go, except drugs, and that scared me even worse.

The first therapy I had to do is related to the symptom for shortness of breath. I was wearing a suit and heels that day because I had been at work earlier in the morning. The doctors wanted me to walk down and back up 10 flights of stairs, then go to a busy patient lobby, find an older, wealthy woman that intimidated me, and sit down and chat with her for a few minutes, until I could re-gain my composure. When I got to the lobby, I sat down next to an older blonde woman, maybe in her 50s, pretty, reserved, reading a magazine.

"Hi there," I said, out of breath and sweating profusely. I felt like a pig, I wanted to take my jacket off but I couldn't because I had nothing underneath it but a camisole.

She looked at me strangely for a moment, then she said hello. She turned back to her magazine.

"How are you today?" I asked.

"I'm fine. How are you?" she responded, shortly.

"I'm good. I'm just on my lunch, on a walk in the stairwell," I lied.

That was part of the deal. I couldn't tell her the reason I was doing it. I just had to gauge her reaction.

"I'm just waiting for my husband to get done with his appointment,"

she said, more warmly now.

I smiled. I asked where she was from, where they were staying.

She told me where they live, about her kids and grandkids, a little bit about their life back home. And then, it was over. I thanked her for the conversation and wished them the best, waving as I walked away.

When I got to the elevator, the doctors were standing there. They were listening to the whole conversation while they waited for me. I told them that was not what I expected to happen, and they confirmed that was exactly what was supposed to happen. I told them to bring on the next one.

Round two was supposed to help with my social anxiety and racing thoughts and lack of focus. In the lobby level of the building that we were in, there was a huge staircase leading to the subway level. There were probably 100 steps and a large atrium overlooking the subway. Along the floor of the lobby level, there were glass panels where people could stand and look down over the edge to the people moving through the subway. Secretly, the staircase had always scared the hell out of me, but I didn't tell them that. Starting at the top of the staircase, I started the walk down the steps with 2 handfuls of change.

When I reached the bottom, I had to "accidentally" drop my handfuls of change onto the hard tile floor, drawing attention to myself. Even better, it was 11:30 in the morning, lunchtime, and one of the busiest times of the day in the subway.

As I made my way down the stairs, my heart started racing and my hands started to sweat about halfway down. I started to worry that I would drop the handfuls too soon. Then I worried that in my 3-inch heels I would trip and fall forward, rolling down the stairs in a beautiful mess. But none of that happens. When I got to the bottom of the stairs, I stood there a moment, observing the people walking by and those sitting in the chairs along the large windows of the atrium. Then, I dropped the coins, making enough noise to draw the attention of just a few of the people that I had just been watching. Otherwise, people went on with their day as if nothing at all just happened. In disbelief, I looked up at the doctors standing above me, watching me at the lobby level. They instructed me to pick up the change and do it again. I was mortified, but did as I was told, like a soldier on the battlefields, doing whatever it takes to save a life.

I walked back up the stairs, out of breath when I got there. I turned around, paused for a few seconds and then made my way back down the stairs. My head was spinning. I was sweating. But I wasn't really afraid this time. When I got to the bottom, I didn't pause at all. I threw the coins down rather than just letting them fall from my hands. Then, I looked around before I bent to pick them up. Within seconds, people who were watching me turned back to whatever it was that they were doing. I started collecting the coins again. Then, a striking, elderly black woman with silver hair pushing a walker came shuffling by me.

"Oh, it's just like pennies from heaven, isn't it?" she said.

I looked up her. She looked like an angel to me. Then I grinned widely at her.

"Yes, something like that," I told her, not sure if I want to laugh or cry.

After I picked up the rest of the coins, I went back up the stairs to tell the doctors what happened. They were amazed. I told them I was ready for the next round of therapy. We took the elevator back up to the doctor's office. They explained that the next and last experiment would help me overcome my fear of dizziness, which I have had all my life. As a young girl and even into my teen years, I would often faint when I became dizzy. In fact, when I was four, I was tested for epilepsy because of the frequency and severity of my fainting spells. Dizziness is by far my worst symptom for bringing on my panic and anxiety.

For this round, the doctors told me they were going to spin me around in a chair, like the rides at an amusement park that I never go on because they make me sick. They told me they would spin me in one direction for 15 seconds, then turn me back the other way for another 15 seconds. They would keep spinning me in this way until I was no longer dizzy and it no longer bothered me to spin in the chair. I looked at them both, smiling but alarmed on the inside like my fight or flight was already kicking in and I hadn't even started yet.

"I'm going to throw up if you make me do this," I looked at them with serious concern on my face. I mean really, who wants to throw up in front of a couple of young handsome male doctors.

"You'll be fine," the older of the two doctors said.

Looking straight at them, I said again, "I'm just telling you now, I'm going to throw up if you make me do this."

"Well, we've been doing this therapy for months, and we haven't had one single person throw up from this experiment," he said. "So if you do, you'll be the first."

Big deal, I thought to myself. I was going to look like an idiot. I wasn't really interested in making history that day.

I sat down in the chair, pulled my legs up, and crossed them in front of me. It was a tight squeeze in the chair, but I actually felt comfortable.

The other doctor started turning me one way, then the other, then back, rotating me for almost 2 minutes. My head was spinning. I was sweating. Most of the time I focused on the wastebasket directly across from me, knowing that I'd have to use it sooner or later. As my dizziness began, I lost focus and my stomach started to turn. The doctor rotating the chair asked me if I was dizzy. I told him that I was. He kept on, spinning me almost another whole minute before I grabbed the sides of the chair.

"I'm going to throw up," I told them.

The same doctor clutched the back of the chair to stop me from spinning. I pulled my feet out from under me and rolled the chair closer to the wastebasket. In seconds, I was throwing up long strings of spaghetti from my lunch until there was nothing left in me. I spit into the basket and turned to look at them.

"See," I said, sarcastically. "I told you I would throw up if you did that to me."

I forced a smile but I was really pissed off. They both laughed as they watched me recover. They told me as we wrapped up the session, that I picked up the therapy faster than anybody they had ever seen.

They told me they had every confidence that I now had the skills that I would need to overcome my panic and anxiety for the rest of my life if I reminded myself of the experiments that I had been subjected to that day. When I left the doctor's office, I actually believed them. I walked out of the building that day and into bright sunshine with every confidence that they were right.

And they were, until the hot summer night in August.

Chapter 28

*T*hat Sunday in August, around 2 a.m., I feel like I am going out of my mind. I can't sleep, my hands are trembling. All I've had is soda crackers and water since Friday night. I call my Dad. I pray that he will answer at this time of night.

"Hey Dad, it's me," I say.

"Well hi there," he says. "What's going on?"

I can't find the words. It's the first time that I've had to say it.

"Brian wants a divorce," I tell him.

God, it hurts like hell to even say it, but it will be better in time, I suppose.

"What do you mean, he wants a divorce?" he asks, as if it's the first time he's really even thought about it, even with all of the shit that has gone on. What a stupid question.

"He came home from work yesterday and told me that he wants a divorce, that this is his second chance at life, and he's going to take it. I have no idea what that means, but that's what he told me," I say.

He says nothing. It feels like forever, but I don't know what else to say now.

"Well, I'm sorry to hear that," he tells me.

"Not as sorry as me," I say, starting to cry.

"Well, maybe it's for the best, Erika," he says.

"I don't know, Dad, but I'm freaking out," I tell him.

"What do you mean, you're freaking out?" he asks.

"Remember when I went through that CBT for anxiety?" I ask. "It's like that. I don't even want to be alive."

There, I said it, finally the truth. All this time, it's me, my fear of not being able to cope without a man. The independent woman in me wondering if I really am as independent as everyone believes me to be, or is it all really a façade? Can I really go through the rest of my life without a man and have it mean anything at all?

"OK, well," he says, pausing, like that changes everything, me saying something like that. "Where are you right now?"

"I'm at home, at the house in the country," I add. Weird, soon enough it will no longer be home to me.

"Do you want me to come out there?" he asks.

"No, you don't need to. But can you just stay on the phone with me for a little while?" I ask.

"Sure I can. Just let me get up out of bed and go somewhere else so your mom can sleep," he says.

I know better than that. My mom will never be able to sleep if she knows that I'm on the phone with my Dad at this time of night. I can hear him mumbling something to her, then getting up, fumbling the phone and moving through the house.

"OK, I'm back," he says. I picture him settling into his recliner in the living room, holding the phone, a blanket over him and his eyes half closed.

"Where are you," I ask?

"Just sitting in the recliner in the living room," he says.

I smile then, the first time in days. I know him so well.

"Dad, what am I gonna do?" I say, the fear filling my voice.

"What do you mean, what are you gonna do?" he asks, his voice raising.

"I mean, with my life? Where am I going to live, and how am I going to have a house and a yard and 3 kids on my own?" I ask, like he really better have the answers.

"Well, first of all, you're going to be fine. Everything is going to be fine," he says. "And you're going to slow down, and just take one day at a time for a while."

He mentions the house I'm going to rent, trying to be positive, trying to change the subject.

"I'm not going to rent it now. This changes everything. I don't want to move twice and if it gets sold then I'll have to move twice. But I don't know how I'm going to buy a house without a down payment,"

I tell him.

"Well, you have some equity in that house," he says.

"Yeah, I know, but I don't get any of that money until we sell it, or Brian decides if he wants to stay there," I say.

There are so many decisions to make, so many things to think about. I feel like I haven't had enough time to absorb all of this myself, and I'm not really prepared to move forward with anything just yet. But I'll have to find somewhere to live and figure out the financing before I can really do anything else.

"For now, I'm going to stay living out here, until I can find a house,"

I tell him, confidently. "I'm tired of moving around all the time. If Brian wants to move out for a while, he can, but I'm going to stay here."

"I think that's a good idea," he confirms.

I'm starting to feel better. I look at the clock. It's 3:30 in the morning.

"Well, so what else do you want to talk about," he says.

"I don't know. I'm good, for now anyway" I say. "I feel like I should let you go, Dad. We've been talking for almost 2 hours."

"Well, whatever," he says. "I'll stay on the line for however long it takes."

"No, I'm good now. Thanks for talking to me about all of this. I love you," I tell him. I haven't said that to my Dad in a really long time.

"Love you too," he says.

For a moment, I feel like I've got everything under control, like I know exactly what I need to do, and tomorrow I'll be ready to do it.

But then, when Brian gets home with the kids later that afternoon, I lose my focus all over again.

Bryce is the first one to walk in the door when they get home from camping on Sunday. I hurry to the mudroom to welcome them home.

"Hey kiddo," I say. "How was camping?"

"It was good, he says. I can tell that he wished I was there.

"Well, that's good," I say, hoping that they all missed me a little while they were gone.

Bennett and Becca come in the door, both looking relieved to see me.

"Did you have fun?" I ask.

They both mumble that they did, probably afraid to admit it to their mom who stayed home alone all weekend. Brian walks in behind them, quiet, and heads toward our bedroom. I'm assuming that he is going to get clothes for the next couple of days while I am there with the kids. I follow him.

"I decided that I'm not going to rent that house after all," I tell him.

"Why," he asks, with an irritation in his voice.

"Well, I don't want to move twice, and if you want a divorce, then I might as well buy a house with my half of the equity in this house," I tell him.

"Well, where are you going to live in the meantime," he asks?

"I'm going to live here. I'll sleep upstairs in our room and you can sleep in the basement," I tell him, like it's non-negotiable.

"Well, why do I have to be the one to sleep in the basement?" he asks.

"Because you're the one who wants the divorce, and if nothing else, you should be the one to move out," I say.

"Well, you don't want to stay here anyway, and you can't afford it either," he shoots back.

"Well, I can afford it if I get alimony from the divorce," threatening him.

"Oh, you would do that, wouldn't you?" he asks.

"What's that supposed to mean?" I ask.

"You have a good job. You shouldn't need any alimony from me," he says.

"Well, lucky for you, I don't want any alimony, and you're right, I don't want to stay here either. This is your dream, not mine. But I'm going to stay living here until we sell the house and I get my equity or until you can pay me my half," I tell him.

"Well, where do you think I'm going to get that kind of money?"

he asks.

"I don't know, either from your Dad or out of the retirement account," I tell him.

"Yeah, whatever. You would make me do that," he says.

"What's that supposed to mean, you ass. I'm entitled to half of that account, you know. We saved that together, during our marriage, and half of it belongs to me," I say, a little bit louder.

"You have got to be kidding me, Erika," he says.

"No, I'm not kidding you," I reassure him.

"I'm staying in this house until you can get me my half of the equity to put down on a house and get a household started, and then I'll leave.

The faster you do it the faster I'll be out of here. If you really want me out of your life for good, then it shouldn't be that big of a problem," I tell him.

He walks out with his overnight bag without saying another word.

Chapter 29

A few days later, I'm sitting at my desk working on my computer when I get a call on my cell phone. It's Marcus. I don't really want to answer it because I don't think any good can come of it, but I haven't really spoken to him all summer, so I answer it.

"Hello," I say.

"Hey Erika, this is Marcus."

"Hey Marcus, what's up?" I ask, curious as to why he would be calling me, especially at work.

"Hey, I'm calling to tell you about something that happened. I should've told you a long time ago, but I didn't."

My stomach turns. Now I'm wondering why in the hell I even answered the phone.

"Well, remember when I went on that hunting trip last fall?" he asks.

"You mean the one to Montana?" I ask.

"Yeah, you guys had a bonfire the night of Janet's birthday and her and the girls came over." he says. "I think they spent the night."

"Yep, I remember," I say. "Yeah, they stayed at our house that night."

"Well, I came home a day earlier from that trip, and Janet and the girls were gone shopping," he explains. "When I got home, there was a message on the answering machine from Brian that he must've left for Janet."

Now my heart is racing. I really want to hang up, or interrupt him and tell him I don't want to hear anymore.

"He was talking about how he couldn't wait for Janet to come over so they could sit under the stars together," he says.

"Marcus, you're kidding me?" I say, interrupting him.

"No, I'm not," he says.

"Well, why didn't you ever tell me this before?" I ask, annoyed with our conversation.

"I don't know," he says. "I just didn't. Right after it happened I told Dave about it, but I didn't tell anyone else until now."

I pause, then, "I don't know what to say, Marcus. I'm glad you're telling me this, I guess, but I can't really do anything about it now. Your divorce is final and mine is in the works."

"Oh, it is?" he asks. "I didn't really know that. Well, yeah, there's a lot of stuff that has happened that I didn't really tell anybody about. I read some e-mails that went back and forth between them too."

Marcus likes to talk, and talk, and talk. He's a jealous guy. He drinks too much. I don't have a lot of respect for him. And I don't really want to hear anymore. All it's going to do is hurt. And I'm hurting enough right now.

"OK, well, thank you for telling me about this, but I don't really feel like there's anything else I can do about it," I say again. "There was some shit that happened in Vegas too that I never told anyone about, the night that we were at Mandalay and you got so drunk. But it's over now. It's just over for me. I hope you can move on. And I'm sorry. I'm sorry about everything."

"Yeah, it's kind of a bad deal," he says.

"Yeah, I know," I say, completely agreeing with him. "Marcus, I've gotta go. I've got to get back to work. Hopefully I'll see you around and we can have a beer together sometime, ok?"

"Yeah, ok, well, I just wanted you to know," he says.

"OK, thanks, bye."

And just when I think it can't hurt any worse than it did, it does.

Chapter 30

The month of August goes by fast. Brian and I try to avoid each other when we're at our house at the same time. For the most part we never see each other. I worry about the kids, hoping that someday they will understand why our marriage was better as a memory. Slowly I'm starting to see it now, like there is a light turning on in my head. All the years of distrust and alcohol and fighting, and physical and emotional abuse are just too much for any marriage. I realize now that if he could look me in the eye every day for almost 2 years and lie to me about having sex with Shelley, then some of the other things that I questioned over the years were all probably true too.

On a Saturday night in the middle of August, there is a street dance going on in town, the same one that started the mess with Shelley two years ago. The last weekend I didn't have the kids is the one where I laid in bed feeling sorry for myself. I didn't want to do that again. I head into town and stop at the Legion for a beer. There are people everywhere and it feels good to be out socializing. I feel like I might be ready to start telling people what is going on. Except that when I walk in the bar, the first person I see is Brian's cousin, Ted.

Ted was the best man in our wedding, the godfather of Becca, the brother of Brian's cousin Bill who hung himself so many years earlier. I figure Ted already knows a little bit about what is going on so it will be easy to tell him about the divorce. I walk over to him while he's talking to another guy from town.

"How are you?" I ask, smiling and grabbing him around the back and giving him a hug.

"Hey, I'm good, woman," he says, hugging me back. "How have you been?"

"Oh, pretty good," I lie. I see his wife Carrie, who was also in our wedding, across the room. I smile and wave.

"Where's Brian?" he asks.

I'm looking over at the bar when he says it. My head shoots back over at him. My God, Brian hasn't told him anything.

"Well, he's got the kids this weekend," trying to smooth it over a little. "I think he took them camping with his mom's family."

"Well, how have you guys been?" he asks, like we're still a family, a cohesive unit.

I just look at him for a moment, staring. I turn my head away because I don't want to have to be the one to say this to him. But it's harder for me than it is for him so I just start.

"I can't believe he hasn't said anything," I say, tears brewing.

Dammit, I thought I was ready for this.

"Said anything about what?" he asks.

"We're getting a divorce, Ted," I tell him.

He just watches my face for a minute.

"What?" he says. He turns away, shaking his head. "You've got to be kidding me."

"No, I'm not," I confirm. "It's the truth."

I tell him the short story, as short as I can make it. From the night with Cole to Brian telling me he wanted a separation, then that he wanted a divorce. We talk about Marcus and Janet's divorce, and our kids, and what we're going to do with the house and the custody.

"So the night of the fishing trip is the night you talked to Cole?" he asks.

"Yeah, I kinda went crazy that night," I say.

"Well, Brian was bawling after he got off the phone with you that night," he says. "He went ballistic. His Dad had to calm him down."

"Yeah, I suppose," I say, "When you get busted after lying to your wife for two fucking years that probably kind of pisses a guy off."

"Yeah, that's a bad deal," he says. "I knew he never told you.

Otherwise you would have been gone."

I just look at him, pissed off.

"God, why didn't anybody tell me?" I ask.

"I'm sorry, Erika. I just couldn't. He's one of my best friends. I couldn't rat him out like that, even for you," he says.

"Yeah, whatever," I say. He knows I'm mad. "I gotta go. You guys take care."

I wave at Carrie again as I'm walking away. What the fuck.

In late August, Brian texts me to ask if I would be interested in submitting our divorce petition online. I laugh out loud at the thought of it. I want him to look me in the eye on every decision that we have to make, knowing that he is the one who started all of this when he fucked that little tramp. Then he asks if I will try mediation. In early September, he schedules a session with a mediator, both of us hoping that we can save some money on the divorce. A few days later, we spend 3 hours in mediation to undo what 13 years of marriage brought together. I am sad at the thought of it, but thrilled that we can behave like adults. I don't want anything from him. I don't want alimony. I don't want child support. I just want him to be a good Dad to our kids. He was a horrible husband, and he will never be a father. A father treats the mother of his children with respect. His opportunity to be a father was lost when he fucked around on me, pushed me around, and lied to me.

Two days later, on the Thursday before Labor Day weekend, I make an offer on a newer house in my hometown. It has 5 bedrooms, 3 bathrooms, great curb appeal, and best of all, it's 2 blocks from my parents' house. The next day the seller accepts my offer and pending Brian getting me my half of the equity in the house, I can move in the following Friday. I am thrilled. I am ready to move on.

Chapter 31

That weekend I celebrate, big time. I'm trying to numb the pain of the past month. I get drunk Friday, Saturday and Sunday. It is just the start of a long downward spiral of sex and booze that lasts until after Christmas. It's the new normal for a while.

That Sunday, I get invited to go canoeing with my parents and the rest of my extended family. We start drinking early. I am drunk by noon. I share a canoe with a cousin of mine who has never paddled an oar a day in his life. We tip over at least 15 times that day. By the end of the trip, my Dad has had enough. He makes me get out of the canoe I am in and get in theirs. We make it back safely but drunk. Then, on the way home, I get into an argument with my mom. I demand that she drop me at Harper's, where I know some of my friends are going to be meeting later that night.

When I stumble in the door, I almost collide with a guy that I have known for most of my marriage, a younger casanova friend of Brian's who has always flirted with me. I want to go home with him from the moment I see him, and I stay close and let him know that I am interested. I figure it is exactly what I need right now to take off the pain of what is likely to end up a nasty divorce. And it's exactly what I need to do to get the second sexual conquest of my life checked off my list. As we leave the bar at the end of the night, I walk with Luke back to his camper. When we get there, we start a fire and keep drinking.

This is the first time as an adult woman that I have openly flirted with a man, let him know my intentions. By 3 a.m. I am tired and have an offer for a ride home. As I'm walking away, Luke follows me and asks where I'm going.

"Well, I can get a ride home if I go right now," I tell him.

"Don't you wanna stay," he asks, lowering his eyes to me and moving in closer.

"Well, I do, but I'm tired. I'm ready for bed," I admit.

He moves a little closer, within a foot of me now.

"What are you doing," I ask.

"I want you to stay, but I don't want to rush you into anything," he tells me.

"Luke," I say, "This is going to happen sooner or later anyway, so it might as well be now, don't you think?"

I look at him, grabbing his hands, holding them tight. I'm cold, shivering. He pulls me into his body to warm me up.

"Well, maybe we should wait until your divorce is final," he suggests.

"I don't know why," I say, my voice raising.

He holds his pointer finger over his mouth, motioning for me to lower my voice, then grabs my hands again. He bends to kiss me. I grab the sides of his face to pull him closer to me and thrust my tongue into his mouth. We are kissing for a moment when he grabs my hand and leads me back toward the campfire. We sit back down for a few minutes and everyone is watching us. His friend Tony gets up from the fire and heads to the camper. I swear there was some unspoken male signal made during that time, but whatever it was, I missed it. There are two women still sitting around the campfire. They offer to give me a ride home. I tell them I'm going to stay. They get up and walk toward their car. We watch the taillights as they head down the gravel road.

When they are gone, Luke stands up from his chair and comes over to me and grabs my hand. He leads me over to their camper. I love the power of the moment, of him leading me, of saying nothing at all and just knowing that we are going to have sex. We walk around the side of the camper and he holds my hand as I crawl up into the driver's seat of the camper. To the left, his friend Tony is snoring on the pull-out bed. I stand beside the bed as Luke brushes against me and walks by to the back of the camper. I follow him. After I step in the room, he grabs the door and pulls it shut behind me.

Then, he places his hand on the sides of my face, kissing me hard.

He smells so amazing. I am taken by his cologne. He puts his hand on my tits and rubs them, gently, like they've never been touched before.

I put my hands at his waist. We're still kissing but then he takes my hands and moves them down over his cock. He is hard, and big. I can already tell that he's bigger than Brian. Nice. I reach inside his pants, trying to get at it, to see what I've got to work with. I pull away from his mouth and smile.

"What?" he says.

I just keep smiling. It feels like this is what I need to move on. What I need to do to get where I'm going now that I'm going to be a divorced, single woman. I move to the button on his pants and undo it, pushing them to the ground. Then I reach my hand inside his boxers, and open them wide at the waist until they fall. Yes, he is definitely bigger than Brian. I am wet. He grabs at the bottom of my shirt and pulls it hard over my head. That turns me on too. I stroke his penis, and he moans, quietly. I push him down on the bed, trying to figure out how his long body is even going to fit across it, but somehow it does. His feet hang over a foot. I look down and laugh. I lay down on my back next to him.

He grabs my boobs again, reaching inside my bra. I reach around my back and undo the clasp and they fall out. His mouth is all over me now, sucking at my nipples until they are hard. I'm surprised I'm not even cold. It's September in the Midwest and its 50 degrees outside.

But right now I am warm, almost hot, and definitely horny. His hands move down to my jeans, unbuttoning them. He doesn't waste any time pulling them off and soon I'm lying there naked in front of a man who is a friend of my soon-to-be ex-husband.

Luke comes down over the top of me, kissing me softly this time.

I open up my legs for him and he slowly eases his penis into me. He is bigger, longer, and thicker. I can feel all of him, all the way inside me.

I realize in that moment that Brian must be average when all this time I thought he was big. I giggle and Luke looks down at me, wondering why.

I tell him I'm nervous. He pushes hard into me and I love it. I grab his ass and pull him into me. We get into a smooth rhythm as I move him in and out. Suddenly he slips out and we both laugh.

"What do you want me to do," he asks.

"What do you mean," I answer back.

"Well, can I shoot it inside you, or not," he asks.

Briefly, I think about where I am in my cycle and realize that we're not even using a condom. Brian had a vasectomy shortly after Becca was born and I haven't had to worry about birth control for 4 years. I'm already a failure at being a single, sexually active woman.

"Yeah, we're good. I'm going to get my period this week," I tell him.

He looks at me strangely, obviously not educated on the ovulation cycle. No surprise for a single guy.

"Are you close?" he asks, kissing me again.

"No, but don't worry about me," I tell him. "I'm too drunk to have an orgasm anyway."

He smiles and gets back into rhythm again, until I can feel sweat starting on his back. I love it. I love the summer time, dripping hot slippery sex in the middle of the night. I think about how we conceived our oldest son that way, and then remind myself to stay in the moment.

God, I thought this would be harder for me to fuck somebody else.

For the first time in my life, I have sex with someone other than my husband. I decide that it's a damn good thing I am drunk. Otherwise, I probably wouldn't be able to go through with it. I'm actually glad that I'm doing this with someone I know. This is the first of many irresponsible but exciting sexual escapades that I will have. And the first of many life lessons I will experience in the ways of the world as a single white female.

The next morning, Luke kisses me on the cheek to wake me.

"I gotta get going. I gotta pick up Boyd this morning," he whispers.

Boyd is his son. He looks just like Luke, a toehead, big blue eyes.

He reminds me of Bennett when he was little. He's tall, a little stocky, friendly.

"OK," I say, rolling over toward him. I smile. Damn, my head hurts.

Naked, I flip my legs over the side of the bed, looking for some semblance of my clothes. I see my shorts, my shirt and bra. My flip-flops are at the front of the camper. Luke is standing there watching me.

"I can't find my thong," I say, smiling.

"Is it in the covers?" he says, laughing. "I think that's the last time I saw them."

"Well, I don't know, but if you find a black lace thong in here, then you'll know it's mine," I say, winking.

I get up from the bed and put on my clothes. He's still watching me. It's odd to have another man watching me get dressed. But it kind of turns me on so I lean in to kiss him.

"Hmm," he says. "Too bad we can't stay longer."

"Yeah, I know," I reply. "Are you sure you have to go?"

He answers by grabbing my hand and leading me to the front of the camper, and out the side door. I'm surprised that his sister is standing out by his car, but I smile and say hello. I don't remember seeing her last night, but I definitely could have. When we get in the car, I sit in the back and she sits in the passenger seat. I'd like to relax all the way home, but for some reason I feel like I have to fill the silence. It's my first lesson in the morning after experience, awkward.

Chapter 32

*T*he following Tuesday is the first day of school. Bryce is 13, starting 8th grade. Bennett is 9, and in 4th grade, and our little baby girl is all of 6 in her first day of the first grade. I take a picture of what will be their last on the front stoop of the house in the country. The day was the last of many actually. That morning, as I was getting ready for work, I walked out of our bathroom into the bedroom as Brian came in after spending the night in the guest room in the basement. I was naked and he was in his boxers. In an unexpected moment, he came toward me and put his arms around me.

"What are you doing?" I ask.

He leans into kiss me then.

"We shouldn't be doing this," I say.

"Why not? You're still my wife," he says as I pull my mouth away.

"It's confusing for the kids," I tell him. And I just fucked one of your friends two days ago.

He grabs my hand and pulls me toward the bed. I am wet, ready to go. He is completely hard. He slides over me and pushes himself inside. As our rhythm is starting, I want him to stop, but I don't know how to say it. I have no idea how long it will be before I can have sex with someone again, but I decide to not waste the opportunity. I think about the sex with Luke two days ago, but Brian is right, he is still my husband and it isn't a crime, even though it somehow feels like one. I want this to be a grudge fuck. That's how I want to remember it, just sex and nothing more. I move out from under him and turn around, doggy style so we could slam into each other. We do, but not for long, maybe 5 minutes, and then it is over.

Three days later, on September 11, I move into my first house as a single woman. I leave almost all of the kids' stuff at the house in the country, hoping to disrupt their lives as little as possible. As if their lives aren't already going to be turned upside down with the divorce. Brian tells me that I can take whatever I want, that I can have everything if I want it. Alicia and I bring just a few boxes and throw whatever we can into them. I take all of the suitcases and fill them with my clothes.

I decide I'm going to need the suitcases when I start traveling again, when I'm back on my feet. We make plans for the furniture that I will take the next day, and pack other little things that we can fit into both our cars. That first night in my new house I am terrified. I was a college-educated woman with a Bachelor's Degree, with 13 years of marriage and a fantastic career on my resume, and I didn't even own a flashlight.

Days later, I get a text from Brian.

Nice, Erika. Sleeping with my friends, now?

What? What do you mean?

You slept with Luke?

What are you talking about?

Don't lie to me.

I'm not. I didn't sleep with Luke.

That's not what I heard.

Well, whatever. You're not even friends with him anymore anyway.

I figure for all of the years of him lying to me, he can get a little dose of it himself. It's none of his damn business. Then later, I'm pinching myself. I should have told him how much longer and thicker and better in bed Luke is than him. What was I thinking?

Chapter 33

Our divorce is final in early December. I'm actually on a trip visiting my sister when I get the news. I'm relieved, but sad. It changes everything. Denise can probably see all of this in my eyes. We're sitting at her house, relaxing. She stops what she's doing to give me a hug. She's been through this before. I feel like she says all the right things.

"You know, it's hard," she says. "You'll pulling apart what 18

years brought together. It's not easy. When I got divorced, it took me four years to get back on my feet again, to feel like I was ready for a relationship, ready to share my life with someone new."

"I feel like I'm never going to be there," I tell her. "I don't know if I ever will be. This is breaking my heart."

"You know what," she says, sensing my change in mood. "We're going out to celebrate. I know this really great little sushi place we can go to, have a sake bomb, make some fun. How does that sound?" she asks, trying to cheer me up.

"Well, first of all, what's a sake bomb?" I ask, my face wincing with a grin. She's got a wild side that scares the hell out of me sometimes.

"Well, it's a Japanese beer dropped into a glass of sake. It will kick your ass, but I think that's just what you need right about now," she tells me.

She's right, I do. I love my sister. She is the best.

"I'm in," I say. "Let's go."

When we get to the restaurant, it's quiet, not real busy, which is nice because I don't want to be in a crowd of people today. The waitress comes over to take our order shortly after we sit down. I look over at Denise, a little apprehensive. I've never had sushi before and I have no idea what to order.

"So what do you think I should get?" I ask her.

She looks at me, puzzled.

"Well, what do you like," she asks.

"I've never even had sushi before," I admit.

"Oh," she says, looking surprised, "Well, let me see," as she looks over the menu.

She orders some sort of combo platter so that I can try a bunch of different things, and two sake bombs. My stomach is in knots. I don't know if I'm more worried about eating sushi, drinking a sake bomb or that my marriage is truly over now. When the waitress brings the sake bombs, I watch Denise as she gets ready to drop the beer bomb into her sake. Clearly, she has done this before. She looks like a professional.

After she drops hers, I pick my beer up, hold it a couple of inches above the glass of sake, and bombs away. The mix of the beer and the sake explodes, overflowing from the glass and onto the table.

"Shit!" I say out loud, backing up from the table. "Leave it to me."

It looks a whole lot like my life, a beautiful mess.

On a Sunday in late January, Brian brings the kids to my house around 5 that night. Becca is the first one in the house, followed by Bennett, and then Bryce. I give them each a kiss on the forehead as they walk in the door. I can see in Bryce's eyes that something is wrong.

I decide to give him a few minutes to get settled before I interrogate him about whatever it is. As the kids are taking off their coats and dropping their backpacks on the mudroom counter, Becca turns to me with a big grin on her face.

"What's that big smile about?" I ask. "Are you happy to see me?"

"Guess what, mom," she says.

"What, babe," I reply.

"Yesterday, Dad and Janet told us that they are dating now," she says, matter-of-factly, and strolls out of the room into the kitchen.

It kind of reminds me of the drink I had in Phoenix. I can feel my face get hot. My hands are shaking. My heart is racing. I look over at Bryce. He's watching me. He purses his lips together like he's disgusted with Becca for dropping the bomb on me. What's disgusting is that my newly titled ex-husband did not have the balls to tell me this himself.

Bennett is trying to be busy doing something in his backpack, but he's listening. I know he's listening.

"Is it true? Your Dad and Janet are dating now?" I ask, tears welling in my eyes.

"Yeah, I guess so," he says, not wanting to be the one to tell me.

"Wow," I say. "Wow," shaking my head.

That's all I've got. I just don't even know what to say to my kids to make this alright. My ex-husband and my best friend. This is gonna be good.

A couple of hours later, I can't stand it anymore. I'm so angry at Brian for making the kids tell me about him and Janet. I suppose my ego is hurt. I suppose I thought he had enough respect for me to tell me himself. But really, how do you tell your ex-wife that you've been fucking her best friend? I decide to call him. While I'm waiting for him to pick up, I get to listen to the song, "I've got my toes in the water, ass in the sand, not a worry in the world, a cold beer in my hand." Lovely, I'm inspired.

When he answers, I start railing into him, "Perfect, Brian. You make the kids tell me that you and Janet are dating? That's nice of you. Did you think of anyone else but yourself when you made that decision?"

"We're not married anymore, Erika," he says. "Why in the world would I need to tell you who I'm dating?"

Our voices are both already screaming.

"Well, she was my best friend, you dumbass," I say. "Don't you think it was hard for them to look me in the eyes and tell me something like that?"

"You're making a big deal out of nothing," he says, laughing at me.

"It's something to the kids. You should have seen their faces when they told me," I say. "How could you not even care about that?"

"Whatever, Erika," he says, trying to blow it off. "You weren't that good of friends anyway."

"Oh really?" I ask. "How long have you two been fucking each other anyway?"

"That's none of your business," he says.

"It's my business when it hurts the kids," I say. "I can't believe you have so little respect for me and for the kids that you would make them do this to me."

"I didn't' make them do anything to you, Erika," he says.

"Did you think they weren't going to come home and tell me about this, like it doesn't change everything for them," I say, yelling into the phone now.

"I don't know," he admits. "I wasn't really worried about it."

"Of course you weren't," I say. "Well, you know what, if you two have all these plans to get married and have kids and live happily ever after, just do it. Don't take your damn sweet time. Hurry up already and just get it over with."

"We're not in any hurry," he says.

"Well, you might as well be in a hurry, because it isn't going to make it any easier on them either way. God, Brian, we're Jenna's godparents, for Christ sakes. How can you do this? Do you have no conscience at all?"

"Are you done now," he shoots back at me.

"No, I'm not done. I'm going to make your lives fucking miserable for doing this. There is no good that will come of this, do you know that? I can't believe that you two are so fucking selfish that you couldn't think of anybody else but yourselves. It makes me sick," I shout back.

When I pause long enough to wait for him to respond, all I hear is busy signal. That cowardly son-of-a-bitch just hung up on me. And then, I go crazy.

Chapter 34

*T*he next day at work, I get an e-mail from a travel company with some great prices on air and hotel packages to pretty much everywhere in the world. It seems like more than a coincidence considering the night I just had. Knowing what's ahead of me when the rest of the world finds out about what's going on with Brian and Janet, I desperately book a three-night trip to Mexico. I'm leaving in 10 days and I'm going alone. I just want to get away, clear my mind, figure out how to handle all of this news. I feel like it's a matter of time before the headlines in our town newspaper read, "Jilted Wife Dies of Broken Heart."

Ten days goes incredibly slowly when your heart is breaking. When the plane touches down in Mexico, the first thing I want to do is get a drink in my hand. Unfortunately, I get side-tracked by a guy who wants me to tour his company's timeshare. I tell him why not. I feel like I've got all the time in the world. He promises it won't take longer than 2

hours, but I know better than that. The last time I toured a timeshare was almost a year ago when we were in Neuvo Vallarta. I was married then. We spent almost an entire day walking around the property, discussing the pricing, negotiating our freebies. I wanted to buy the timeshare. Brian thought it was a waste of a day. He was probably already making some other plans for his life without me.

The guy gives me a certificate for a free shuttle to the resort for the following morning. When the van arrives, I chat with the driver in broken Spanish to find out more about the city.

"Hola," I say. "Donde es name?"

"Juan," he says, a thick accent.

Oh, this is probably going to be a tough conversatioin.

"Wats urrs?" he asks.

"Maria," I lie. I just want to be someone else for a few days., maybe forever. Maria sounds good to me.

"Wherrre you fram, Maria?" he asks.

"The Midwest. All my life." I say. "How 'bout you?" I ask.

"Dominican," he says. "Puerto Plata."

"Aah, Dominican. Nice.

It's crazy little pieces of someone that help me put together part of who they are. Before long, we're at the resort. He runs around the side of the van and grabs my hand to help me out.

"Gracias, Juan" I say, smiling.

When I enter the lobby of the resort, I am overwhelmed by the height of the ceiling and the beautiful, shining tile floors. The room is a rotunda. It's spilling with people everywhere. I walk toward the front desk and share the certificate that I have. The clerk points me to a desk to the left. When I approach, the woman at the desk, named Ahna, smiles and grabs the certificate from me. She gets on her phone and makes a request for a salesperson. She gestures for me to have a seat in the chairs on the other side of the desk, near a fountain. A few minutes later, someone touches me on the shoulder. I turn around to find a striking woman with reddish hair, a few freckles and deep set green eyes. She is wearing a pair of khakis and a royal blue polo shirt with the name of the timeshare company on it. She smiles at me warmly and reaches out her hand to shake mine.

"Hi there," she says. "Are you Erika?"

I stand up, taking her hand in mine, "Yes, I am," I tell her.

"I'm Michelle. Nice to meet you," she says.

I immediately like her, so I say, "You too."

She explains that she's going to give me a tour of the resort that we're at, then take me over to a new sister resort that is being built down the coastline. While we walk, she tells me she is a single mom, divorced, with a son in his early 20s. She lived in the Midwest all her life until she got divorced. Then she came to Mexico for a vacation, bought a timeshare, and was recruited to do sales. She left the Midwest after her son graduated from high school. Our conversation just flows. I tell her my story, the basics. Throughout the tour, I have little moments of absolutely loving what I see. I think Michelle knows it, but I don't want to say so. I start thinking about what it would be like to buy a timeshare right now. I didn't book this vacation to do that, but it feels like it might be the right time to do it. The idea of buying a timeshare by myself as a single woman is exciting, empowering. And buying at a resort that is just being developed is even better. If I can get a good deal now, I might be able to turn it over in a couple of years and make some money on it.

When we finish the tour, Michelle takes me back to the first resort.

We sit down at a table in their make-shift "office" that is a restaurant at night. There are other salespeople and "clients" scattered all over the room. She gets me a Corona with a lime. She talks to me about the available rooms, the seasons, the pricing, all new stuff to me. As I'm sitting there listening, I look out the windows at the open sea in front of me. It's the beauty of wave upon wave, crashing in on the shore. I've seen the ocean before, but it's nothing like this. Michelle is talking to me then, but whatever it is, I missed it.

"You know," I say, "I really just want to go sit on the beach, put my toes in the sand, get a drink in my hand."

She smiles and says, "I gotcha."

We both stand up, and Michelle turns toward the door. I follow her out of the restaurant and out into the open air. It feels good to be back in the wind again. We walk down a set of stairs that leads to the beach. She walks with me out onto the sand, about halfway to the ocean, maybe 20 yards to the water. It's soothing for me. I just want to sit and enjoy it for a moment, so I do. Michelle sits next to me.

"So, whattya think?" she asks.

"About what," I reply.

"This," she says. "Is this something that you're interested in, something that you want to think about it, come back later. What are you thinking?"

"Well, I can tell you right now, I can't afford the top end of what you're offering," I tell her. "I'm a single mom with three kids, no alimony, no child support, and I can't afford to spend that on a timeshare right now."

"Well, what about something like $24,000," she counter offers.

"Yeah, no, probably not," I shoot back. "Something more like 18 would work."

She looks at me, smiling. I think she likes me.

"Let me go back and check with my sales lead and see what we can do," she says, standing up. "Are you ready for another drink?"

"Si," I tell her. "How about a margarita this time, on the rocks, ok?

"Sure, sounds good," she says, winking. "I might have one too."

As she walks away, I lay back on the sand, digging my toes in as deep as they will go. The top sand is hot, but I dig in deeply enough to get to the cold layer below. It feels good. I watch people around me.

They are walking, running, standing, sitting. Some look at me and smile as they pass. Others watch the waves and the water. I feel more alive than I have in a long, long time. Michelle comes back with a margarita in one hand and some papers in the other. She hands me the margarita.

"Gracias," I say.

"Hey, well," she says. "I'm shocked, but he went for it."

"Went for what?" I ask.

"The $18,000. That's a great deal, you know," she tells me.

She sits down next to me and hands me the contract. She reviews everything, line by line. It just sounds like blah, blah, blah, to me. I'm buying a timeshare. It's gonna be mine. What else do I need to know.

When she's done, I briefly look it over.

"Time for my autograph now, I guess, huh?" I say.

"Yeah, your autograph," she says, laughing.

"I'm serious," I tell her. "I'm going to be famous someday."

She just laughs again, then says, "OK, let me take this back and get it approved, and bring you another margarita to celebrate."

"Sounds good," I say, as I wait for her to return.

When she comes back again 15 minutes later, she hands me another margarita, congratulates me, and tells me she wants to take me out for drinks to celebrate. Perfect. In one hand, I've got a freshly signed timeshare contract, and in the other, a margarita, on the rocks. And a life that is just about the same.

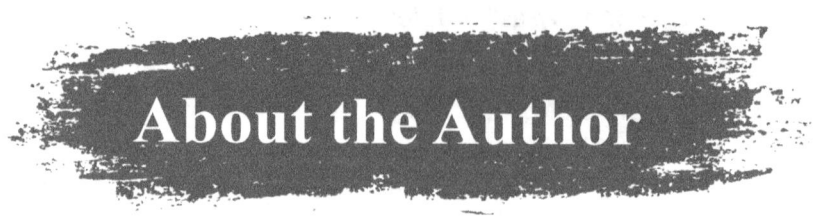

About the Author

Erika Daniels is the pen name that represents a single, divorced, mother of three who lives in the boondocks of the Midwest. All my life I have wanted to write a book, but I never felt like I had the life experience to do it, until now. Unfortunately, I had to earn it the hard way.

I started this book 3 days before I left on a 10-day vacation to Mexico. I had written 3,000 words at that time. By the time the plane touched down at home, I had written over 33,000. Within a week, the book was done, just 30 days later. I had no idea how easily the words would come.

Thanks to my first best friend, Jess, who grew up down the street from me and was the very first person I shared this work with. As kids, we rode our bikes and swam at the pool, and when the sun went down we played "Kick the Can" and "Ghosts in the Graveyard," stealing kisses and claiming our first boyfriends. We lived in a neighborhood full of boys, which I'm still convinced is what made us the smart, strong and amazing women we are today. She read the book in just over 6 hours.

In her feedback to me, she told me she sees a sequel in my future. I say, only if it's a love story.

Thanks to my kids, for their love and patience with me, as I have evolved into more of myself and away from the woman and mother I never wanted to be.

Thanks to a mother and father who have seen my worst reflection and love me anyway.

Thanks to God for unanswered prayers. I have always been a spiritual person, but during this experience I started going back to church, lectoring, and teaching religious education classes. I truly believe everything happens for a reason, and the contents of this book are proof of that.

My hope is to help other women like myself, women who have survived abuse, addiction, dishonesty, disrespect or the infidelity of a partner. May this book provide the courage to change the things you can, knowing that someday you may experience a better life.

www.ingramcontent.com/pod-product-compliance
Lightning Source LLC
Chambersburg PA
CBHW060804120626
46557CB00001B/82